The Disappearance of
Representative Government

The Disappearance of Representative Government

A CALIFORNIA SOLUTION

Robert T. Monagan

COMSTOCK BONANZA PRESS

GRASS VALLEY, CALIFORNIA

ISBN 0-933994-10-9

Contents

ABOUT THE AUTHOR   vi
ACKNOWLEDGMENT   vii
Introduction   1
Prologue   6
The Class of 1960   16
Representative Government   24
Citizen Representatives   34
Reapportionment   44
Campaign Financing   63
Initiatives   71
Power to the Unelected   86
Regulation Without Representation   95
Impact of Modern Media   107
Conclusions and Recommendations   119
   Solution One: Reapportionment   123
   Solution Two: Legislative Operations   132
   Solution Three: Campaign Financing   141
   Solution Four: Initiative Process   147
Epilogue   152
Monagan's Laws   159
PROPOSED CONSTITUTIONAL AMENDMENTS
   A. *To Change the Method of Redistricting* 161
   B. *Relating to Legislative Sessions,*
      Salary and Expenses   165
   C. *Relating to Campaign Contributions*   167
   D. *Relating to the Initiative Process*   173
INDEX   181

About the Author

THE MONAGAN POLITICAL LINEAGE

1951—Committee for Reapportionment, San
Joaquin County, California.

1952—Eisenhower for President Campaign
Director, San Joaquin County, California.

1953–1954—Administrative Assistant to California
Congressman Leroy Johnson.

1958–1960—City Councilman, Tracy, California.

1960—Mayor of Tracy, California.

1961–1973—Assemblyman, California State Legislature.
Speaker of the Assembly, 1969–1970.
Minority Leader, 1965–1968; 1971–1974.
President National Conference of State
Legislative Leaders.
Member Council of State Governments.
Chairman Presidential Electors for California, 1968,
1972.
Co-Chairman Re-elect Nixon Committee for
California, 1972.

1973–1974—Assistant Secretary for Congressional and
Inter-Governmental Affairs, U.S. Department of
Transportation (appointed by President Nixon).

1978—Member U.S. Department of Transportation Safety
Advisory Committee (appointed by President Ford).

1983—Member President's Advisory Committee on Private
Sector Initiatives (appointed by President Reagan).

1984—Member, and present Chairman, California State
World Trade Commission (appointed by Governor
Deukmejian).

Acknowledgements

To my wife, Ione, acknowledgment and recognition must come first. Without her love, support, understanding, and tolerance nothing in my life would have been possible—and certainly not this book. (10:29)

My appreciation to David Comstock, who provided editing to bring clarity to what I was attempting to write. He knew what I was trying to communicate, and thus was able to mix my thoughts with his experience and skill for the benefit of readers, if there turn out to be any.

I have been most fortunate to have survived life itself, and a public life in addition, for a long time. I am twice blessed because of that survival. There is one difficulty. It is not possible for me to acknowledge here all of those people that I have been associated with over those years. Hundreds of friends, associates, and people that I have worked for, who have worked for me, worked with me —and even some who worked against me—have helped mold, shape, support, and sustain a long and enjoyable life and career.

I never had to walk any road alone. Thank you all for walking with me.

Introduction

"Politics is not a bad profession. If you succeed, there are many rewards; if you disgrace yourself you can always write a book." —Ronald Reagan

This book is about "representative government." There is a great misconception among the people that we still have representative government in our country. They are wrong. At least, we no longer have representative government as the founding fathers of this country created it in 1787.

They would be alarmed (maybe even enough to send out Paul Revere on another ride to alert the populace!) if they could see what has happened to the system they carefully crafted in Philadelphia over 200 years ago.

I am alarmed!

After nearly three decades of personal involvement in our system of government, I would suggest that we are on the edge of losing the last vestiges of that precious representative process that has served us so well for over two centuries.

Fortunately, it may not be too late for us to return to a *citizen* form of representation, or at least to a modern form of it. That is, it is not too late if we act quickly. If we do not make changes, we can soon forget about representative government.

Anyone who isn't startled by the scandal of campaign financing, the distortion of the initiative process, the rapaciousness of reapportionment, the decline of the political parties, and the loss of citizen representatives simply isn't paying attention to what is happening.

Those aren't the only issues, but awareness of these and others, and discussion of them, should convince any thinking person that we must start making some significant changes.

My observations in the pages that follow are not academic; they are based upon personal experience and involvement. They are based on the real political world, but they are not partisan.

I have had the good fortune to have participated in government and politics for over 35 years. That involvement included elective, appointive, and volunteer positions in local, state, and federal government. It also included partisan and non-partisan participation. Thus my conclusions are based upon real-life experiences in the political system—not textbook or academic conclusions.

I am intensely concerned about the future of our government processes. This book is not a biography. The references to and reminiscences about my career, are mentioned only to lend credence to my concerns and suggestions. Paralleling "Honest Abe," it is not my intent to approach this other than with charity for all and malice toward none. This is not intended as an attack upon politicians, past or present. It serves no purpose to look for the "faulters," and it's more important to look at the faults. I am just deeply concerned.

If we put aside the sensational exploits of a few in public office, it is the "system" that is on trial, not necessarily the participants in that system. Our present representatives may be no better or worse than those who created the system in the first place. There is, however, a decided difference in the manner in which they operate and function within that system.

It is time to reconsider where we stand today in terms of representative government. If you agree with me that we want to restore and preserve it, we must act quickly.

I am afraid that if our founding fathers could see how we have corrupted the system they crafted so well, they might start another revolution. For that is what I am writing about—a *political* revolution, conducted by modern patriots, to save "representative" government for ourselves.

This is not to suggest that what those founding fathers thought was necessary at the time always will apply to today's circumstances and conditions. The Constitution was not meant to be a static document, because the conditions and concerns and needs of the people are not static. Justice Oliver Wendell Holmes once said, "The Constitution is an experiment, as all life is an experiment." There are four major concerns that will be discussed here:

1. The decline of the citizen representative.
2. The inability of the legislature to fairly reapportion itself.
3. The "political arms race" for campaign funds.
4. The misuse of the initiative process.

These are the primary issues to be addressed, and for which reforms will be suggested. Subsequent chapters will deal with some related causes and effects. Then I'll describe the corrective actions I think we must begin to take, where and when and how. My goal (and I hope yours, too, when you hear what I have to say) is to stimulate Californians into action at the state level.

A simple but interrelated approach is needed to address the fundamental concerns. Piecemeal solutions will not solve our problems. In our system of government and politics, the art of the possible is the objective—we cannot hope to make the whole system letter perfect.

Years ago, when our football team had played a

particularly bad game, the coach would announce that it was "back to fundamentals" for the team. That, in part, is what this book is about. We should remind ourselves what representative government is all about and take a hard look at the problems that have arisen within that system.

A famous French marshal once asked his gardener to plant a favorite tree. "But, monsieur," replied the gardener, "that tree takes a hundred years to grow."

"Then we have no time to waste," declared the marshal. "Plant it this afternoon."

Prologue

"What is past is prologue."

A first time visitor to Washington D.C. was riding around the nation's Capitol in a taxicab one day when the taxi headed up Pennsylvania Avenue. As they drove past the National Archives, the visitor looked at the top facade of the building and noted the quotation chiseled into the marble, "What is past is prologue." He turned to the driver and asked, "What does that mean?" The driver replied, "You ain't seen nothing yet!"

So a little recollection of the past may be necessary to prepare for the future. In this instance, some of my past may be helpful in understanding how I came to write this book, and perhaps expose the foundation for the conclusions I have reached about representative government today and my concerns about its future.

I certainly don't know everything about the subject of representative government, or about its current problems, but I do know a lot about it. If experience is a good teacher, I should be well taught by now. For the past 38 years I have either been in appointive or elective office, or at least on the close periphery of politics and government. That experience has included elective, appointed, and volunteer activity in local, state, and Federal government.

My involvement in politics and government was somewhat accidental (my critics might even say haphazard), and certainly not in the current manner of young people who embark on a political or governmental career. That in itself is one of the present-day problems I will be discussing. Unlike today's crop of politicians, I had lots of career ideas in mind, but politics wasn't one of them.

In fact, I have to admit that my interest in politics was nil when I became eligible to vote for the first time. When the registrar of voters asked in what party I wished to register, I hardly knew what to reply. My father was a Democrat, and Franklin Roosevelt was the popular Democrat President of the day, so I responded by registering as a Democrat.

My first partisan involvement occurred in 1952, when I was the young manager of the Tracy Chamber of Commerce. A friend of mine was the chairman of the Eisenhower for President Committee in San Joaquin County, and because of my experience in organizing activities, he asked me to be the campaign manager for the committee.

My first response was that my Chamber of

Commerce directors would object to such partisan activity. He asked if I would take the job if he could get me a leave of absence, and I said I would. He did, and I did, and that's how I got my political start.

From there on my career went downhill or uphill, as the case may be. At the conclusion of the Eisenhower campaign, Congressman Leroy Johnson, a Republican from Stockton, called me one day and asked me to be his administrative assistant in Washington, D.C. That sounded exciting, so I uprooted my extremely loyal and understanding wife and three children, and we trekked across the country.

It was a truly exhilarating experience to be in the nation's Capitol for the very first time. Attending the inauguration of Eisenhower was an historic moment, but I had many other equally memorable first impressions of things political and governmental.

There is a lot of truth in the old saying that people should neither watch sausage being made nor politics in action. My first visit to the U.S. Senate Chamber was a good example. I was very impressed to sit in the gallery and listen to that great orator from Minnesota, Senator Hubert Humphrey, deliver a long and impassioned speech on federal aid to education. He certainly got my attention. It was well that he did, for I was the only person in the gallery, and Hubert was the only senator in the chamber.

Humphrey was noted for being long winded, but he was humorous about himself in this regard. He said he was invited once to give a ten-minute speech, but confessed that he couldn't do it. He claimed it took him ten minutes to say good morning to his wife, Muriel.

My Washington experience was short, lasting less than two years, but it was valuable, and made me acutely aware of what representative government was all about.

I recall very vividly the two congressmen whose offices adjoined that of Congressman Johnson. One was Bob Poage from Texas, who was a dirt farmer, boots, cowboy hat, et al. He didn't have a strong educational background, but he was chairman of the House Agriculture Committee. On the other side was Congressman Cliff Cole from New York. This erudite man, who had a doctorate in science, was chairman of what later became the House Science and Technology Committee. These two were as opposite as you could ever imagine—and they represented constituencies that differed in much the same way. Each was reflective of his own community and its interests.

It was not an easy task in those days to be an administrative assistant to a congressman. It was six months in Washington, and then pack bag, baggage, wife, and children into the station wagon to drive back home to open the district office. Six months there, and then reverse the process. It was an exciting life, but it put a strain on the young Monagan family. Becaue I had no deep-rooted political ambitions, when a new opportunity appeared, I jumped at the chance to go home.

I had returned to Tracy to enter the insurance business, and because community activities offer good entree for selling insurance, I was soon involved in many of them—Rotary Club, Boy Scouts, United Way, church, you name it. In any small town, the person who will serve as chairman or president, or take a leadership role in such groups is always welcome. It wasn't insightful of me to accept such positions, but before long my "accidental" political career took another turn. A great number of local people urged me to run for the city council in Tracy. (Isn't it strange that politicians are always being "urged" by a "great" number of others to run for office?) Nevertheless, I ran, was elected to the council, and before long became mayor.

I thought that might be the pinnacle of my political career.

Being "Mayor" can be fairly prestigious and ego-satisfying, although mayors in this country are not treated with the same respect as they are, say, in England. There, when the mayor is introduced, it is "His Excellency, the Mayor," and when he comes into the room, it is "His Worship, the Mayor." When our officials enter the room it's just "My God, the Mayor."

Then another political accident befell me. Frank Hoyt, the county supervisor from our district, privately informed me he wasn't going to run for reelection the following year, and he suggested I prepare to run in his place.

The district was a natural for me. I was well known in the area, and having nearly a year to lay the ground work before other candidates learned of his decision would give me an important head start. Being the Mayor of Tracy didn't hurt either.

In those days, local politics was not as partisan as it has since become (it might not be a bad idea to return to that less partisan local government). Although I was now well-known as a Republican, other community and civic involvements tended to minimize that factor. Besides I had been elected by the citizens of Tracy to their city council, and the partisan registration in that locality was 69% Democratic.

I decided to begin a quiet campaign. Before long I had informal committees in place throughout the supervisorial district, and I was busily circulating in many non-political guises. It is likely that I would have been elected to the board of supervisors in the 1960 election, but once again fate intervened.

One morning I went to the State Capitol (for only the second time in my life) to testify before a water committee on behalf of the Delta Water Users Association, of which I was general manager. On this same day my wife, Ione, received a phone call in Tracy from our long-time friend, Democratic Assemblyman Bill Biddick. Bill told Ione that in two days he would announce that he would not be running for reelection. Because of our long friendship (and partisan politics be damned), he wanted me to know about his decision 24 hours ahead of other potential candidates.

Ione tracked me down in Sacramento, and upon returning home that night, I phoned my closest associates, all of whom were preparing to support me in the supervisorial contest. I wanted their opinions about shifting from a contest that was a virtual cinch to win, to a race where the odds were heavily against me. The district registration was 65% Democratic, and it would be a partisan contest. No one really expected a Republican ever to capture that district. And yet, I don't recall now why or how, we made the foolhardy decision to shift our efforts to the Assembly contest.

Bill Biddick and I shared many things in common. We both graduated from the College of the Pacific in Stockton (now the University of the Pacific), where we were fraternity brothers and partners in campus politics. Bill was a class ahead of me. During his junior year he ran for student body president, and I was his campaign manager. The next year, I ran for that office and he was my campaign manager. We won both elections.

But in later politics our paths diverged, for Bill Biddick entered the real political world as a Democrat, and was twice elected to the State Assembly. He was a highly regarded representative and would easily have been reelected as long as he chose to run in his district. But Bill wanted to be a judge, and a vacancy had occurred on the Superior Court in Stockton.

He could have asked Governor Edmund G. "Pat" Brown to appoint him, but decided that he would be better off without that endorsement, for Brown's popularity was declining. Instead, he decided to run for the position without temporary advantage as the incumbent. That choice was indicative of the high character of Bill Biddick.

Biddick's announcement of his decision not to run and my own announcement to go for his seat appeared in the same edition of the local papers—no one in either party was prepared, and it is a wonder that charges of skullduggery were never made.

"It is better to be lucky than skillful," says an

old adage, and it applied in my case. Although some Republican opposition developed, there was little question that I would win my party's nomination. That was an important advantage, for I could plan the campaign and nurture modest campaign contributions for the entire election period from February to November.

But the luck came mostly from the Democrat side, where Biddick's unexpected decision left the Democrats totally unprepared. Nevertheless, they anticipated no real threat, confident their party could win the seat regardless of which Democrat was nominated. Six Democrats jumped into the contest. At the party convention no one garnered the necessary votes to win party endorsement, so all of them ran in the primary.

I breezed through the Republican primary, but a bruising contest between the Democrats brought an unexpected result: the person I considered their third strongest won. Had either of two other candidates won the Democratic primary, I doubt that I would have won in the general election. The "accidental politician" again.

It was a tough election—the toughest in my political career, but I think I was helped by my numerical disadvantage. The Democrats were lulled into complacency, never expecting it was possible a Republican could win the district. This one barely did. When the votes were counted, I had won a narrow victory of 2826 votes out of 88,239 cast. Another "political accident" had occurred, for I was the only Republican in the state to capture a seat previously held by a Democrat. In politics, it really is better to be lucky than skillful.

I want to make Judge Biddick's political record absolutely clear: as a loyal Democrat he did not support me in this election. The head start he gave me was out of sheer friendship. On the other hand, he never did much to help any of my opponents. After becoming a judge, his partisan politics diminished and became something of his past.

The Class of 1960

"There may be said to be two classes of people in the world: those who constantly divide the people of the world into two classes, and those who do not."
—Robert Benchley

In the election of November 1960, there were nine new assemblymen (and "men" is appropriate usage, since there were no women elected in this class). That was a relatively small number of new members, and nothing like the onslaught of 33 and 34 in the following classes of 1962 and 1964.

Each of the nine ran in districts where there was no incumbent to challenge, and except in my case all were replacing members of the same party. There were five Democrats and four Republicans in the Class of '60. The other eight had relatively easy times winning their races in districts that were generally safe for their party.

Five of my classmates were Democrats: Jimmy Hicks from Sacramento, John Knox from Richmond, Bob Leggett from Vallejo, Jim Mills from San Diego, and Jack Casey from Bakersfield. The three Republicans besides myself included Bill Bagley from San Rafael, Hugh Flournoy from Claremont, and Gordon Cologne from Indio.

Why talk about the Class of '60? Only to show how they differed from people who are becoming our representatives today. The members of this (and earlier classes) were much closer to being citizens of their communities. They had other professions and occupations to participate in and to resume when their legislative careers ended. None started out as interns or staff persons with the objective of running for office. All were ambitious, interested in politics and government, but they were involved successfully in other careers before running for office.

They were *citizen* representatives: a labor official, four lawyers, three teachers, and an insurance agent, and in those days all went back to their respective professions when sessions ended.

My own non-political pursuits were just as checkered as my political activity. Teaching, coaching, association manager, insurance and real estate broker, lobbyist, and a few other occupations were all interspersed with political involvement. From this checkered career I have developed a profound fear that we have lost the essential elements of the representative form of government that we inherited from our founding fathers. It is time, perhaps even past time, for us to carefully review where we are heading, and make some significant changes.

It was an unusual class from the very beginning. For one thing, it was the last class to be among those who were sworn into office on a holiday. The State Constitution at that time provided for the legislature to convene its new session on the first Monday in January, and in 1962 this happened to fall on New Year's Day. The Constitution was later amended and the legislature now meets on the first Monday *after* the first day of January.

There is something to be said for longevity: it certainly beats the alternative in life. This is also true in politics. The longer this group remained on the Sacramento scene, the more prominent its members became. The record book gives strong support to my belief that this class was one of the "classiest" ever to come to the Assembly. Some might disagree, but the achievements of this group are very noteworthy.

Two members dropped out of the class early. Unfortunately, Jimmy Hicks died during his first year in office, and Bob Leggett became a member of Congress following the 1961 reapportionment. The others stayed in the Assembly for a longer time, and created a remarkable record.

Jim Mills early became chairman of the Assembly Rules Committee, a potent position in running the affairs of that body, and was later elected to the

State Senate, where he became President Pro Tempore.

Jack Knox spent his entire legislative career in the Assembly. He became a premier legislator, and one of the state's real experts on local government. For a long time he was also the Speaker Pro Tempore. The Speaker Pro Tempore is a principal assistant to the Speaker, and Knox presided over Assembly sessions a great deal of the time on behalf of the Speaker.

Jack Casey also spent his legislative career in Assembly, and served as chairman of the Social Welfare Committee. Because of his professional career in education, he was expert in matters in this field as well. After retiring from office, Casey later died.

Hugh Flournoy, a college professor prior to his election, assumed a key role in education legislation. In 1966, having decided to retire from the legislature, he was persuaded by his friends to run for state controller. The story about how he was convinced to run for this office probably should be told by someone else, since I was not an eyewitness. It was my good luck, or not, as the case may be, to have returned to my district after the session for some sort of meeting. But even secondhand it is an interesting piece of political legerdemain.

A mixed bag of Republican and Democrat lawmakers had gathered together for a festive night in Sacramento after a relatively raucous day in the Assembly. The party was lively and lengthy, I am told, and the end result was that the group, under the minor influence of distilled spirits, persuaded Flournoy to enter the race for state controller.

The deadline for filing for the office was 5 p.m. the next day. By the time the party broke up, it *was* the next day and money for the filing fee had been raised, including contributions from some Democrats who will remain unnamed, to protect them from their own party friends. The ubiquitous Bill Bagley, I am informed, led the charge to gather the necessary signatures.

I received an early morning phone call at my home in Tracy from Flournoy, who sought my opinion about the sudden decision. But it was too late for any advice. The glow of the night's activities had not yet diminished, and by the time he called the deed was decided and done.

Shortly thereafter, all those who had been present seemed to retire from the scene. None would volunteer or be convinced to chair Flournoy's campaign, so I, who had been blameless, was the lucky one to draw this assignment.

All is well that ends well, so they say, and in the Reagan election sweep of that year, Flournoy was pulled to victory, but with the narrowest margin of any Republican elected to constitutional office that year.

He served as state controller for eight years. His outstanding record in that office propelled him into the Republican nomination for governor in 1974. He lost a close election to Jerry Brown, and many observers say that had the election period been two weeks longer he would have defeated Brown.

Gordon Cologne, a lawyer by profession, highlighted his career in that field and became a leading legislative expert on water issues. He ran for and was elected to the state senate, where he gained great prominence dealing with water questions. He and Assemblyman Carley Porter were co-authors of the Porter-Cologne Act, a primary California water law. Governor Reagan later appointed him to the San Diego Appellate Court, and Cologne has since retired from that position.

Bill Bagley is an attorney by profession, a profession that is frequently put down by many people—including me on some occasions. It is always worth a chuckle from audiences—but not lawyers—to say, "if all lawyers were laid end to end, it would be a good thing."

Bagley, of course, is the exception, and if he had devoted himself to a career in law, he would have made an outstanding record in that profession. Instead, he jumped into politics. Bagley ultimately gave up his assembly seat to run for the Republican party nomination for state controller in 1974, and unfortunately did not win the primary election.

He was then appointed by President Jerry Ford to be the first chairman of the Federal Commodity Futures Trading Commission, a newly created regulatory agency. Bagley returned to California after his term ended to begin practicing law. (Why are doctors and lawyers always practicing?)

When George Deukmejian was first elected governor, he appointed Bagley to the State Public Utilities Commission. When that term was over he returned to legal practice and simultaneously was appointed chairman of the California Transportation Commission by Deukmejian. And after that tour of duty, Deukmejian again tapped him to be a member of the prestigious University of California Board of Regents. Bagley was an honored graduate of that institution.

It is not possible for me to talk about the Class of 1960 without mentioning another individual inextricably related to, but not technically a member of, this group elected in 1960.

Jack Veneman joined the class following a special election in January of 1962 and immediately became an integral part of the group. His contributions to our collective accomplishments were outstanding. He left the legislature to accept appointment as Under-Secretary of Health, Education, and Welfare when Richard Nixon was elected President in 1968.

At the end of Nixon's first term, Veneman left

Washington to return to California to start his own consulting business, and to begin a campaign for the Republican nomination for lieutenant governor. Regretfully for the people of California, he did not win that primary election. When Nixon resigned from the Presidency, and Nelson Rockefeller was selected by President Ford to be Vice President, Rockefeller asked Veneman to return to Washington to become his counsellor.

At the end of that service, he again returned to California and the private sector. Most unfortunately for the people he served so well in public office, and most deeply for those of us who were his friends, he died prematurely in April 1982.

The remaining members of the Class of 1960 have created a Tontine. This arrangement calls for the group to meet upon the death of any member, and to observe the sad occasion by consuming the contents of a bottle of rare cognac in memory of the departed friend. An outsider was commissioned to obtain this case of fine cognac, and keep it in his care and protection until needed for another sad meeting. John Parkhurst, a friend of the group and former legislative advocate for then Pacific Tel and Tel, is that trusted soul.

Representative Government

"What have you given us, Mr. Franklin?"

The history of our form of representative government is exciting, and needs to be refreshed in our minds when we discuss this subject.

Benjamin Franklin is alleged to have been the first of the delegates to emerge from a hot and humid building in Philadelphia on September 17, 1787. Inside that building the Constitutional Convention had been struggling to complete its work. A citizen approached him and asked, "What have you given us, Mr. Franklin?" He responded, "A republic, if you can keep it."

Ah! "A republic!" That is what it is all about.

A republic if we can keep it. Our frequent friend, Webster's Dictionary, clearly defines a republic: "A state in which the supreme power rests in the body of citizens entitled to vote and is exercised by representatives chosen directly or indirectly by them."

Haunted by the specter of the monarchy they had so recently overthrown, concerned about the efficacy of "pure" democracy, the delegates had struggled for a long time to reach the compromise delineated in our Constitution. It was a precarious agreement that they reached. It prompted Franklin to caution that it was a great and precious victory for the people "if you can keep it."

Lord Acton's famous quotation, "Power corrupts; absolute power corrupts absolutely," might very well have been the underlying thought when our system of government was being formed. The gentlemen (there were no ladies present) sitting in the halls of the Pennsylvania State House were "powerful." Make no mistake about that. The 55 delegates to the convention, although designated by their respective legislatures, were there because they were potent forces in their states. They were not necessarily elected so much as "self-selected"; "self-anointed" rather than appointed.

They were expected to draft "The Constitution of the United States of America." During their deliberations, the subject of "power," and where it would rest, took up a major portion of the debate from May to September of 1787. Those assembled knew all about power.

Having once overthrown a monarchy, they were not in any mood to create anything remotely related to a kingdom. On the other hand, they didn't want to establish a government without *any* powers. The delegates struggled mightily over the division of governmental powers between the states and a central authority. That central authority was divided further by debate over a "Federal" or "National" arrangement.

The ultimate conclusion was to draft the unique and tenuous system of checks and balances (tenuous if you call survival for over 200 years by that name). It was *division* of power, not elimination of power, that was the hallmark of this experiment. How was power to be divided between the legislative, judicial, and executive branches of federal government; and between the states and the new federal government? How much power would be assigned to each? This approach to the division of such powers had never been tried before. There was no textbook to turn to; no precedents in history to review. They were cultivating new governmental and political ground.

Now those powers might have been construed to be equal, but equal only in a momentary sense. For once created, stronger power moved by degrees back and forth when there were strong Presidents, potent legislative forces, or activist courts. Each of these was able to be dominant for the moment or a short duration.

President Franklin Roosevelt was a "power"

President for a very long period of time. He was able to dictate to the Congress, and even to some degree to the Supreme Court. The Supreme Court has on occasion been the dominate player, especially the Court presided over by Chief Justice Earl Warren. That Court took the lead and the power in at least two paramount issues: school desegregation (Brown vs. School Board) and the one-man one-vote question (Baker vs. Carr).

There have been instances when the Congress was in the power lead, but those occasions were less noticeable and less frequent. Does this say something about our representative form of government?

Well, what did we have created for us?

We have 3 levels of government—local, state, and federal.

We have 3 branches of government—legislative, executive, and judicial.

We have 2 houses of the legislature.

IT'S A WONDER ANYTHING GETS DONE!

The unique compromise governmental system that we have depends upon a magic glue to hold it together. That glue is a representative system, and that system depends upon our ability to continue to select people who truly represent us. The danger today is that too many persons, despite good will and good intentions, seem to be representing themselves.

There is a great misunderstanding, or lack of understanding, among our citizenry about this representative system. A political trivia question quickly brings this to mind. Ask someone for whom he or she voted in the last Presidential election, and the most likely response will be the name of a principal contestant for that office.

Of course, such an answer would be wrong.

They voted (if they voted at all, and half of the voting age citizenry did not) for someone to "represent" them in electing a President. The process is that voters select Presidential Electors to meet and vote on their behalf. These electors, although designated to vote for a particular candidate, are not legally bound to do so, even though they are nominally representing *us*.

I have twice been a Presidential elector; in the elections of 1968 and 1972 I represented the electorate for Richard Nixon. In 1972, I was chairman of a representative group that numbered 45, the number of Electoral College votes to which California was entitled. We met in the Capitol at Sacramento in formal session to cast our votes and forward them to U.S. House of Representatives, to be tabulated with those from other states.

Although the world *knew* we had elected Nixon President immediately after election day, it was not official until this representative process was completed. And in fact, there is always the possibility that Presidential electors will not vote the way they are expected to, despite a moral—but not legal—obligation to do so. In the 1972 election, Congressman John Schmitz, a California elector, refused to vote for Richard Nixon.

There are other misconceptions and erosions in our system of representative government. Some of these have to do with the approach to governing that many of our representatives have adopted.

While I was in the state legislature I recall Father Leo McAllister, the Chaplain of the Assembly, giving a morning prayer that I have always remembered. (Yes, every session of the Congress and our state legislature is opened with a prayer. One day, a mother and son were visiting the Congress and heard the Chaplain give the opening prayer. The little boy asked his mother, "Why is he praying for the congressmen?" His mother replied, "He is not praying for the congressmen, he is praying for the country!")

One morning Father McAllister urged us to be more like "thermostats" and less like "thermometers." He said it was our role not to just test the political-wind direction by raising a wet finger into the air, but to help set the political temperature of the people. Nowadays, our representatives aren't even inclined to test the wind before acting, because our society has become so complex, the issues so controversial, and our population so split into special-interest groups, that a clear signal can't be discerned. Which, in a sense, makes it possible for representatives to ignore their constituents.

Thomas Carlyle once wrote, "Popular opinion is the greatest lie in the world." We have finally reached the epitome in poll-taking. In a recent poll, 100% of the people were recorded as "undecided" or "don't know."

The practice followed by many legislators of sending out questionnaires to their constituents raises a further question: how many representatives are truly seeking responses, and how many are simply using them to keep their names fresh in the minds of voters? If you look at the questions asked, it's hard to escape the latter conclusion, for they seem to fall into such categories as: When did you stop beating your wife? Are you for taxes or against them? Or, if you can understand this question, don't bother to respond!

One legislator asked: "What do you think is the most important thing the legislature should do?" One of his constituents replied: "Recently married, wife pregnant, just moved into a new home and broke. I don't know anything about anything. Neither does my wife. Thanks for asking." So much for putting one's finger in the air to check political windage.

It is probably fair to say that many of the most important issues today are very divisive, and the margins are narrow between one segment of the public and another. On some issues we may divide 55–45, on others it may be more like 51–49. In addition, we have divided ourselves into various special-interest groups, covering a wide range of concerns, such as protecting the environment, pro- and anti-abortion, creationism vs. evolution, funding for education, animal-rights, labor unions, business and industry, fair trade, protectionism, ethnic groups, disarmament, military preparedness, and many others. In fact, the division between Republicans and Democrats is a piece of cake compared with divisions among the special-interest groups.

These groups have power—*negative* power. Almost all have enough political muscle to prevent things from happening, but by themselves, none have the power to cause *positive* things to happen. Consequently, for something to happen, our representatives must step in and make the tough decisions. But do they? Not very often.

Unfortunately, these divisions in society make it easier for legislators to delay or avoid the issue by pleading that there is no consensus among the public. They forget who is supposed to be the "mind" of the public. One constituent who understood this wrote to his representative:

"I was given this card to urge you to support a bill I know nothing about. Since I have complete confidence in your judgement, I will use it instead to wish you a happy birthday."

Horace Greeley held decided opinions on the subject of representative government. Never inclined to be wishy-washy, he once said, "I do not regret having braved public opinion when I knew it was wrong, and was sure it would be merciless."

Or as movie mogul Sam Goldwyn put it, "I don't want any yes men around me. I want every body to tell me the truth, even if it costs them their jobs."

At present there is no incentive to make our representatives address these difficult and troubling issues, because to confront them poses the genuine risk of being dismissed from office. But isn't that a risk that is essential, if representative government is to work properly?

We have a gridlock of political response to the problems facing our nation and our state. *We have a political policy failure*, caused by the diminution of true, or nearly true, representative democracy. Because our track record has been fairly good for a couple of centuries, it is tempting to think we can continue to muddle through to some resolution of the dilemmas facing us. But careful examination of that track record shows we are going downhill at an accelerating rate.

If we want some resolution of the problems

confronting us, we will have to make some changes in the system of representative government as it has evolved. We must look at the history of representative government, understand what it is supposed to be, see what has happened to it, decide if we want it back again, and if the answer is yes, *do something* about it.

In following chapters there will be a discussion of these matters, along with recommendations of changes I think we should make, at least in the state of California.

Citizen Representatives

"The people will be represented; they ought therefore to choose the representatives. The requisite in actual representation should sympathize with their constituents, should think as they think and feel as they feel, and for those purposes should be resident among them." —George Mason, Virginia delegate to the Constitutional Convention

We have come a long way from George Mason's admonition about the kind of representatives we should have. One of the more distressing developments since then has been the change from "citizen representatives" to what might better be termed "professional legislators."

Citizen representation seems to have vanished from the scene, despite the founding fathers' belief that an elected official not only should represent a community of voters, but also be a member of that constituency.

Now our representatives are hardly known in the area they represent. They live in Washington, D.C., or in the state capital. They become homeowners.

Their children go to school there. As a result, they are more representative of the area in which they live than the one they are supposed to serve. They become "visitors" to their constituents, and their visitations are apt to occur with greater frequency as election day draws closer.

The original idea was that our officials, as representatives who worked and lived in the communities they served, would bring a broad base of knowledge and experience to their deliberations. Ironically, the trend today is in the opposite direction. The idea of "full-time" legislators that has permeated the system is not what the founding fathers envisioned. Earlier legislators visited the capitol to represent the views and concerns of the people who elected them, but they lived in the districts where those people also resided.

Now there is nothing deleterious about serving your constituents with all of your time. But there is a mistaken idea that *all* of that time should be in formal session, or at least in the capitol. Our current representatives would be far more effective in carrying out their duties if they spent a significant portion of time in their home districts.

It gets a sure laugh from audiences when a speaker suggests we ought to pay our legislators more money when they're *not* in session than the other way around. Which, of course, is a play upon the ancient and frequently quoted court decision that said, "no man's life, liberty, or property is safe while the legislature is in session."

I don't mean to be cynical, for these are contentious problems we ask our representatives to solve. The point is that they would learn more *about* those problems, understand better the views of their constituents, and could help people understand the complexities of issues, if they spent more time in their home districts.

The founding fathers were the functioning leaders of their communities; not just leaders in the capitol. They were often more likely to be the best educated, best informed people in the community. They felt a responsibility not only to respect the wishes of the people, but to help them in reaching responsible decisions. They neither wanted to be "professional" servants or "lifetime" employees of the people. Most would have preferred to stay home and take care of their business, farming, or professional interests.

Now we have too many representatives who want to be "professional" (translation: a semantical device for seeking larger compensation) and work full time because it is the best job that they will ever have. But it was meant not to be a job, full- or part-time, but an act of public service. If we are to have professional legislators, we should hire, not elect them. (It is reasonable to suppose that few of the present incumbents would be hired under that arrangement.)

John C. Calhoun, who served as Vice President of the United States and played many other distinguished roles, gave a speech on July 13, 1835, in which he said, "The very essence of a free government consists in considering offices as public trusts, bestowed for the good of the country and not for the benefit of an individual or a party."

There is also a dangerous trend underway in which an increasing number of people reach office by first becoming legislative aides. Charles Price and Charles Bell, writing in the *California Journal* of April 1989, on the subject of "Lawyer-legislators: The Capitol's Endangered Species," observed that in 1959 no member of the California Legislature was reported as having been a former legislative aide. By 1989 that had changed, and 11% of the representatives were former legislative aides.

Now, don't jump to a hasty conclusion about these legislative aides; they are generally well educated, intelligent, and have learned about the legislative process and government by excellent on-the-job training. If they were go back to the local district and get jobs as teachers, lawyers, business persons, or in any other vocation, becoming dues-paying citizens of the community in the process, then they would be better qualified to serve as citizen representatives.

But as it now stands, they are more apt to be "selected" than elected, for with the backing of the incumbent whom they will replace, heavy endorsement by the Sacramento or Washington party powers, and endowed with generous campaign funds, staff assistance, and professional campaign artists, they have a tremendous head start over other candidates. The result is little choice for the citizens.

These former staff members frequently fall into the category of never having been a real part of the community they have been elected to represent, and because of the current "full-time professional" concept, they never become strongly involved in their home community. Those representatives who had been active members of their communities before seeking office at least had some prior knowledge of the home district.

If all this sounds like finding fault with our representatives, it is only partially so. They have permitted, or, in some instances, instigated this situation. Generally speaking, they have found this system already in place, and they quite naturally took advantage of it. But I am a strong advocate for changing the system so these folks can once again become "citizen" representatives.

A July 25, 1989, column by Dan Walters, the *Sacramento Bee* political observer and writer, strikes at the very heart of the problem. Walters wrote: ". . . perceived problems with the Legislature are merely symptoms of an institutional disease that has developed over the past two decades. *That is its alienation from those whom it is supposed to serve.*"

The italics are mine, added to emphasize that this is the most salient problem with which we must deal. Failure to turn that alienation around will result in the loss of the foundation of representative government. Of course, Walters is not very popular with incumbent legislators. Umbrage is usually taken by the current office holders when someone writes or comments in a critical manner about the present status of our political system.

But neither Walters nor I or the others who write about this problem are as concerned about the people involved as we are about the system in which they operate. Present office holders are all too apt to vigorously (and erroneously) rise to the defense of the system, and thus serve their own cause poorly. It only raises suspicion about their motive in defending a system that is not working well. Walter's primary point was that either we must abolish the full-time legislature and return to a part-time body, or we should modify it severely.

The late State Senator George Miller, Jr., father of Congressman George Miller (both liberal Democrats from Contra Costa County), always had an applicable quip for almost any situation. The crusty, but extremely likable elder Miller was a powerful member of the legislature in his day, and whenever anyone complained that some legislative action was not fair, Miller always replied, "Show me in the rule books where it says we have to be fair."

Well, it is also not in the Constitution, or any statute or rule of the legislature that the legislator is "full-time." True, the legislature does seem to be *meeting* all the time, and some legislators do devote their entire working effort to the position, but there is nothing in legal concrete that says this should be the case.

The idea that our state representatives would serve full time developed from several circumstances. Once upon a time some legislative leaders (and I was one of them) put forth the idea that the legislature could deal with problems more effectively and efficiently by changing the legislative format to biennial sessions. We thought this would enable legislators to function more effectively and efficiently within the existing system, and did not imagine it would encourage them to become mere visitors in their home districts.

I know there were some legislators who wanted

the office to become one of total occupation (with commensurate compensation), and who supported the proposal for those reasons, and there were other more reasoned arguments being made by experienced observers who cautioned against this development.

Lobbyists are not necessarily held in high regard, and their motivations may be considered suspect. They are employed to look after their clients' interests, of course, but in most cases they also are long-time observers of the legislative process (many are former legislators themselves), and are greatly concerned about the democratic process and how it works.

I thought this proposal would not automatically lead to a full-time system, which I opposed even then. But many from the lobbying fraternity, led by the redoubtable James D. Garibaldi, argued that "full time" would result, like it or not. Garibaldi, dean of the lobbying community in Sacramento, and still one of the most respected (some translate that into "powerful") legislative advocates, constantly reminds me of our misconception.

Some of the underground argument in favor of this biennial session saw in it a way to get increased pay for legislators. Although I believe lawmakers should be adequately recompensed, this shouldn't be offered as an excuse for full-time positions.

In fact, the debate really ought to concern itself with whether the legislature should be in formal session nearly all the time, and not whether its members devote all or part time to their tasks. Addressing that problem and changing it can do a great deal of good in turning our legislators back into citizen representatives.

It was not too long ago that formal sessions of the legislature adjourned or recessed to let representatives go home to their districts. Most did return to a business, profession, or farm, and even those who had retired from their previous vocations went home to be available to their constituents. If they didn't have a job to return to, they could work in their district legislative offices.

These recesses also provided an opportunity for what were referred to as "interim studies." Legislative committees could hold hearings at the scene of the problem they were discussing, or at least in an atmosphere where citizens could be heard from in a reasonable manner.

The evolution of the full-time legislator parallels the growth in the length of legislative sessions. The longer the session, the stronger the appeal for higher compensation. Unfortunately, with less time available to go home and be confronted by constituents, the representative becomes farther removed from the realities of the community. There is a line that goes, "If you want to lead the band, you have to face the music." Some of our legislators prefer not to be in the district to face the music, which can be especially discordant after the long and continuing absence of a leader.

We must put together a system that brings our representatives closer to those they represent. We really need a return to citizen representatives. Our republic cannot successfully survive a situation where its legislatures are alienated from those whom they are supposed to serve.

Reapportionment

"The foxes in the hen houses"

One of the greatest experiences that I've had in politics and government is to work with young people and see them grow, develop, and succeed. Of course, you will see a great number of them if you survive long enough. And I have seen a lot of them.

On reflecting about these fine people, it sometimes seems I must be getting old. It's not that I think I'm old, but I do find that when I think about insurance policies these days it is less likely to be about major medical policies, and more in search of minor miracle policies.

One of those fine young people I have been associated with is T. Anthony Quinn. When I first became Speaker, and thus entitled to additional staff, one of those hired was Tony Quinn, although my first impression of him was not all that favorable. Tony was young, quiet, and without a very imposing background of experience, other than the fact that he had worked in a congressional campaign in Texas for a candidate who was a family friend of Tony's parents (the candidate was George Bush, who also went on to gain some notoriety).

Nevertheless, Tony's parents lived in my district, and Tony had been recommended by my chief of staff, Jerry Simpson, so I decided to give him a chance. He turned out to be an excellent writer, researcher, and was insightful in dealing with issues.

One of those issues was reapportionment, and he is now one of the recognized experts on that question. I am indebted to him for his advice and information over the years, but I am most in debt to him for letting me read an early draft of his book, *Carving Up California: A History of Redistricting, 1951–1984.*

Of the many causes (and results, as we shall see) of the loss of representative government, none is more significant than reapportionment. The process of drawing district boundaries for our system of representation has done more to bring about the decline in appropriate representation than any other single factor. What reapportionment is and how it impacts our lives is hardly understood by the voters at all. It is imperative that they learn quickly.

One of the ways for the people to understand what reapportionment is all about is to comprehend what is the meaning of the word most apt to be heard from now until the next reapportionment: GERRYMANDERING.

It would be worthwhile for all citizens who are concerned about politics and representative government to read the recently released monograph by Dr. Leroy Hardy. Hardy is an expert in reapportionment issues, and currently is a Senior Research Associate at Claremont McKenna College's Rose Institute.

The monograph is entitled, *The Gerrymander: Origin, Conception, and Re-emergence.* Gerrymandering, as we use the expression today, got its early usage in 1812. How much credit or discredit Eldridge Gerry should receive for the origin of the term is much debated, but he is stuck with it.

Gerry was the governor of Massachusetts when a hotly contested reapportionment occured. One district was grossly distorted for certain political benefits, and on viewing it critics said it looked like a "salamander." Because of Gerry's involvment in the process the term became colloquialized as "gerrymander."

Gerry, in addition to being the governor of Massachusetts, had been a signer of the Declaration of Independence, and a delegate to the Constitutional Convention.

California, beginning in 1966 and after the Supreme Court decision, "One man, one vote", has its own style of gerrymandering. An example of

The infamous Gerrymander. (From Hardy, *The Gerry-mander: Origin, Conception and Re-emergence*, The Rose Institute, 1990.)

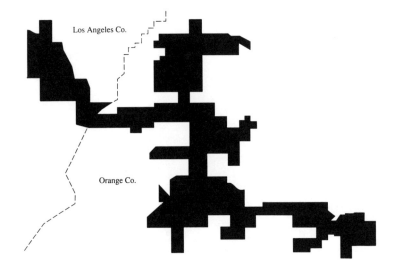

The "Corydor," an Assembly district proposed in 1971 by the California legislature, but vetoed by the governor. (From Hardy, *The Gerrymander: Origin, Conception and Re-emergence*, The Rose Institute, 1990.)

California distortions of the process, the best example is the district in Southern California proposed for a prominent democratic office holder, Assemblyman Ken Cory. It became known as the "Corydor" district. Cory was able to advance from the Assembly to become the two-term State Controller for California.

Gerrymander or Corydors, whatever the term applied, it is extremely important for the people to understand what can happen to representative government under reapportionment scheming.

Except for the 1981 reapportionment, I played a part in all the redistricting battles covered in Quinn's book. That's how I cut my teeth in politics, and these experiences form the basis for most of my conclusions about the issue.

As I said in an earlier chapter, in 1951 I was a young Chamber of Commerce manager in Tracy, California. I had not been involved in any even remotely political activity. By that time I had changed my registration from Democrat to Republican, but that was done in a fit of pique over Franklin Roosevelt's decision to run for a fourth term as President. My decision had nothing to do with Roosevelt's policies or political philosophy, it was the result of my feeling that no one should serve in that office so long that it became a virtual monopoly.

Because I was serving with the U.S. Coast

Guard at the time, on board a Coast Guard cutter in the Aleutian Islands of Alaska, it was a comparatively easy thing to do—I went to the ship's clerk, asked for the forms, changed my registration, and I never gave it another thought until a long time later.

The Constitution of the State of California at that time called for Assembly Districts to be comprised of entire counties, singularly or within whole counties. San Joaquin County, following the 1950 census, was mathematically entitled to about one and a half districts, but had two current assemblymen.

When the 1951 legislature met to consider reapportionment, the future of representation for San Joaquin County was in doubt. Reapportionment could leave San Joaquin County with two representatives, or cut the number to one.

Strange as it might seem to those who have never witnessed such a phenomenon, Republicans had a majority in the legislature, and a Republican was governor. Thus it would seem that the Republicans ought to have been in total control. But reapportionment historically has been more of a personal than a partisan issue. As Quinn accurately points out in his book, Republicans were the first to interject extensive "gerrymandering" into California's political lexicon and practice in 1951.

One of the county's two assemblymen was a

Democrat and the other a Republican. It was going to be a close call as to which way the legislature would respond to the county's dilemma. The county's community leaders decided to put on a full court press, with Republicans and Democrats joining forces in the fight to retain both seats.

Because I had been involved in many civic and community activities, I was called upon to help lead the county in this non-partisan effort. We headed for Sacramento to plead our case. The hearing was perfunctory, I was to learn later when I became familiar with the legislative process, but this was my first visit to the State Capitol. I didn't set foot in it again until I attended an Assembly Water Committee meeting in 1960, the same year I became a candidate for the Assembly.

Needless to report, our efforts went for naught, and it was the Republican majority in the legislature which took the extra seat away from San Joaquin County and gave it to another part of the state where the chances of party success were better. I returned to my job and forgot about reapportionment until I was a member of the legislature myself.

Well, what is reapportionment all about? It goes back to the gigantic battles that occurred in Philadelphia in 1787. One of the major battles of the convention was fought over the issue of representation. A Congress composed of a Senate and House? How many senators per state? A House determined by population? When population grew or if new states were admitteded, how would they be represented?

The fight over these questions was long and labored. The "Great Compromise" was reached, granting each state two members in the Senate, which would offset the effect of proportional representation in the House of Representatives. A census would be taken every ten years so the number of representatives could be recalculated with accuracy.

(Census takers relate many humorous stories based upon the experience of getting this information. One is about the man who answered the knock on his front door and a stranger said, "Sir, I'm the census taker and Congress has sent us across the country to determine how many people live in the United States." A look of puzzlement was reflected in the man's face, and he said, "I'm sorry you came to ask me, because I haven't the slightest idea!")

After this calculation was made and the number of districts in each state determined, it was left to the respective states to draw the lines for their own districts. "State's rights" was a powerful factor at that time, and no one anticipated the mischief that could and would result from this decision.

In her great book, *Miracle at Philadelphia*,

Catherine Drinker Bowen quotes one delegate, John Dickinson, as saying, "If the General Government should be left dependent on the State legislatures, it would be happy for us if we had never met in this room." His words were prophetic, at least for California, where our state constitution provides for the legislature to reapportion congressional, state senate, and assembly districts.

It was not an awesome or onerous task for our state legislature to do this before 1951, according to Tony Quinn. Two essential factors limited the legislature's options when designing districts: (1) the California Constitution forced legislators to deal essentially with whole counties; (2) this in turn meant they were not strictly bound to achieve absolute equality of numbers between districts. Within these limits they could play games all right, and they did; but it was more difficult to arbitrarily deal with personalities and political parties.

Quinn cautions that reapportionment must be understood in terms of what it *is not*. He says, "it is not about representative government, not merely the mathematical exercise of redistributing people among electoral districts, and indeed reapportionment is not even about reapportionment: it is about politics."

I would agree with those comments, with one major exception: I emphatically believe that, since 1951, reapportionment *is* about representative government. Why? Because of a decision by the Supreme Court, which I believe has resulted in the diminution of what the makers of the Constitution had in mind for "representation."

The court action was the celebrated (or infamous) "one-man one-vote" decision by the Earl Warren Supreme Court. It was odd that a Californian, familiar with the nature of our state government, would lead the charge in this decision. It wiped out provisions of our state constitution which tied districts to county boundaries, and in many ways has led to a startling distortion of the spirit of "The Great Compromise" of the Federal Constitutional Convention, as it related to state's rights.

The Supreme Court, seeking to address a severe and sincere problem of persons who were being deprived of their right to vote and thus be represented, addressed the problem in the wrong way. Though intended to eliminate barriers to voting, the decision actually has led to the creation of new barriers which prevent many voters from being *fairly represented.*

The bottom line of that decision, and subsequent rulings, is that, for all intents and purposes, the only remaining legal hurdle left when drawing district lines is the distressing factor of "mathematical perfection." If the numbers add up, nothing else matters—no consideration of existing political subdivisions, geographical barriers, communities of interest, or ethnical relationships—and certainly no thought of a state's right to define its own system of government.

States are even prevented from emulating a system like that of the federal government! Our own California "little federal" system was outlawed. The bones of Jefferson, Adams, Franklin, Washington, et al, must have been rattling in their graves when the Court rendered this decision.

And worst result of all, and either totally unanticipated or ignored by the Court, this decision opened up the candy store for legislators, who now can distribute the goodies any way they please, only subject to challenge if the sweets aren't divided equally among themselves.

In California, it produced a field day for legislators in charge of the new process. The late Congressman Phil Burton, Democrat from San Francisco, was the master of them all. I knew he was a Houdini of reapportionment when I first became acquainted with him in 1961, after my election to the Assembly.

Veneman, Bagley, Flournoy, and Monagan didn't sit at Burton's knee, but we did spend long hours with him, discussing the subject of redistricting and learning the facts of political life. In those days, very few legislators had their families in Sacramento, the full-time syndrome having not yet come on the scene. Early in the session, we would be in Sacramento from Monday to Wednesday, or perhaps until Thursday noon. As the sessions moved along, we stayed until Thursday night; then to Friday afternoon. On the last few days of the session, when the hard-to-avoid legislative crunch was on, we might be there the entire week.

Many nights, after sessions were over, we would run into Burton at the Top of the El Mirador, a hotel across the street from the Capitol, and a favorite watering hole for legislators. This was before the age of computers, but Burton was a human computer. His fertile mind contained megabytes of information relating to reapportionment. He knew more about the political composition, voter proclivities, economic and ethnical characteristics of any given district than any legislator, including the representative of that district. He could rattle off the probable voter change if districts were moved this way or that, without referring to any source except what was in his own brain.

Burton may not have been totally accurate in every detail, but nobody was equipped to challenge his facts. And once Burton and others were given the computers to play with, and the Democratic party controlled the votes in the Congress and the state legislature, the ball game was over.

I don't know exactly when the application of the

computer to reapportionment studies first occurred, but I do know when it first came to my attention. In my files I have the December 1964 issue of *American Behavioral Scientist*, containing an article by Edward Forrest of Computer Applications, Inc., in which he describes a computer program "able to incorporate several political considerations in its creation of equal-population legislative districts."

Not long after reading that article, I met Dr. Alan Heslop, who was experimenting with applications of the computer to reapportionment, and was developing programs to use the information being accumulated (Heslop is now Dean of Rose Institute of State and Local Government at Claremont McKenna College). Voting and registration records were being merged with census information to develop tools for drawing districts to suit the draftsman's delight and specifications. And I do mean "draw." For one who didn't know what a computer was in those days, it was an amazing sight to watch a machine translate statistical abstracts into lines on a map.

It was my first introduction into the world of nearly instantaneous information manipulation; and this was over 20 years ago. The magic of the technology today, coupled with the mountains of information available from records and the U.S. Census, gives fantastic tools to the reapportioners.

They know almost everything about us—how we

are registered, how we might be inclined to vote, the size of our families, our ethnic backgrounds, our economic status, how many cars we have—even how many toilets we have (though I am hard pressed to surmise how that latter factor might influence voting patterns; perhaps that's where people are more apt to do their reading).

When you superimpose this capacity upon the one-man one-vote decision, the door is open to unlimited mischief. With incumbents doing the drawing, and California Democrats controlling the legislative process at present (and for the foreseeable future), you can see where this all leads. (Please remember what I said earlier about Republicans started this gerrymandering in our state—they would do it again, if they had the chance.)

The districts are drawn, with ingenuity and the computer, to satisfy the desire of incumbents to have safe districts, and the desire of the controlling party to stay in power, without regard to the effect upon logical representation for the people. Is it any wonder that this method of defining districts results in representatives who don't represent us?

In the 1988 election to select 45 members of Congress, 20 state senators, and 80 members of the Assembly—a total of 125 elections to decide our representatives—115 incumbents (from both parties) were re-elected, *including one who was dead!* Seven non-incumbents won, but they were elected to fill seats previously held by members of the same party. Only three incumbents were defeated.

Before the 1988 general election, Assembly Speaker Willie Brown remarked, "In the last several elections, over half of the state's eligible voters did not show up at the polls." Brown went on, "A representative form of government cannot survive when most of its citizens do not bother to exercise the franchise."

Many citizens do not even bother to register to vote, let alone vote. But why should they? It is preordained, in over 90% of elections for Senators, Assemblypersons, or Congresspersons, the people who are supposed to represent us in government, that the incumbents will win, *whether or not we go to the polls and vote.* Is it any wonder that people are disinterested, when in the races most vital to their interests they have no real choice?

And although Speaker Brown decries the low level of voter turnout, he was a primary player in the distorted reapportionments of 1971 and 1981 that produced the malrepresentation that leads to voter disinterest.

It is very safe to say that if we let the legislature continue to have total sway in the 1991 reapportionment, Speaker Brown will again be a key participant. Would he change the reapportionment decisions to allow more fair and competitive districts? Not likely! Disregarding any partisan considerations he might have, it's unlikely he would permit the City and County of San Francisco to lose its present over-representation in order to create "fair" districts throughout the state.

Yakov Smirnoff, the Soviet-born comedian who is now a U.S. citizen, jokingly commented on the advantages of participating in the traditional Russian election process: "You don't have to compare candidates, follow campaigns, listen to debates."

Unhappily, that is not too different from our own situation under the present reapportionment process. We don't even need to show up at the polls anymore, under these conditions. I frequently offer to wager that I can predict, with 90% accuracy, who will be elected to the Congress, State Senate, and Assembly, well in advance of the next election. So far I have had no takers.

In the "Intelligence" section of *Parade* magazine, July 9, 1989, an article, "Tired of Losing," described a group of defeated congressional candidates who have banded together to try to diminish the windfalls of incumbency. They cited the elections of 1986 and 1988 when more than 95% of the House members who ran were returned to office. This group proposed a number of reforms that would give non-incumbents better chances to get elected. One suggestion was to limit the number of terms one could serve, something I don't advocate, because there are better ways to solve this dilemma, which I'll discuss later. Unfortunately, they did not propose any changes in the reapportionment process.

I am not one of those who believes incumbency is automatically bad. Actually, in most cases the incumbents are (as they claim) more experienced, knowledgeable, and better qualified than their opponents. But having said that, it is only fair to point out that this occurs because no strong candidates will emerge to oppose them because of the near-impossibility of defeating an incumbent.

If we reapportion correctly—or should I say fairly in the eyes of the electorate, and not necessarily in the eyes of incumbents or the political parties—we will have a great number more districts in which any candidate has at least a mathematical chance to win. The creation of more competitive districts doesn't mean incumbents won't be reelected. However, it's less likely this will occur at anything like the present 90% rate.

The purpose of bringing reform to the reapportionment process is not to "get" incumbents, at least in my way of thinking. In most instances the incumbent is apt to be the better qualified candidate. He or she will be familiar with the issues, and have had considerable other experience. If the districts were divided fairly, a challenger at least would have an opportunity to conduct a campaign with some chance of success. As it stands now, even a good candidate with adequate financial support stands little chance against an incumbent.

But creation of competitive districts is precisely what those who control the reapportionment process hope to avoid. Because, when forced to compete on equal footing, an incumbent actually suffers from certain disadvantages. He or she has a voting record that can be challenged by opponents, and because it is extensive, dealing with many controversial issues, and easily distorted in a campaign, the incumbent can be put on the defensive.

That in part is why current representatives have a difficult time coming to grips with significant issues. But what *we* need in our representatives is a willingness to take stands on the issues, even controversial ones, without regard to whether or not they will be reelected because of positions they take. We can't expect that kind of performance from a full-time professional—but we have every right to expect it from a citizen representative.

Campaign Financing

"Money, money money." —Napoleon Bonaparte

Ovid is quoted as writing, "How little you know about the age you live in, if you think that honey is sweeter than cash in hand."

When Napoleon Bonaparte was asked what were the three most important elements in winning a war, he replied, "Money, money, and money!"

Jesse Marvin Unruh was often quoted as saying that "money is the mother's milk of politics."

I don't know where or how Unruh conjured up his quotation, probably after reading about Napoleon and Ovid, but his comment has become the common currency of conversation whenever people discuss politics these days. He can't be blamed for all that has happened in the way money and politics are interrelated these days, but he was certainly perceptive enough to turn money to his political advantage.

Politics and money, money, and money, has become a significant issue. Bonaparte's rejoinder about war and money describes what is happening in politics. If our representative government is being ridiculed and held in high suspicion, it is because of the magnitude of the dollars involved in political campaigns today.

Some are quick to say that "money is the root of all political evil," to paraphrase an old expression. I don't necessarily subscribe to that school of thought, but money certainly is one of the root causes for the loss of representative government in America, and it has reinforced a growing loss of confidence in our ability to obtain honest government.

The old joke about having the finest legislatures "that money can buy" is no longer just a funny line—too many people are beginning to believe it. On the eve of the legislature's 1989 summer recess, a *Sacramento Bee* story read: "For the people of California, a few critics said, that means their wallets are safe for another month."

Some would interpret this as meaning the recess would frustrate the legislature's ability to damage us by means of legislative action; but for those persons who are regular targets for campaign contributions, the recess also meant temporary relief from a steady stream of fund-raising events. Does it seem odd that most fund-raisers occur when the legislature is in session and important issues are being voted upon?

If every other odorous factor about the money in politics was ignored, the fact that our representa-

We resent the implication that we can be bought!

Just because lobbyists spent $83 million on us in 1989 and

also spent millions more in campaign contributions and speaking fees!!!

We never said we couldn't be rented, however!

Cartoon courtesy of Dennis Renault and the *Sacramento Bee*.

tives spend an inordinate amount of their time raising money to stay in office would remain as an imposing loss. In 1988 a record $61.6 million was raised and spent on campaigns for the California legislature. That is 8 percent more than in 1986, and 180 percent more than just ten years ago. It is *four thousand percent* more than was spent in 1960, when I first ran for the Assembly. It is predicted that this year's legislative races will cost an average of $1 million apiece—and if not this year, certainly by 1992 that will be true.

In 1960 I spent a grand total of $15,000 for my primary and general campaigns, which at that time was the largest amount ever spent for a campaign in San Joaquin County. Even though I had editorial support from every newspaper in the district, nearly every paper printed some caustic comment about what seemed to them an excessive sum. And why was it $15,000? Because that was all we could raise in 1960.

By itself, the enormous amount of money raised and spent for elections does not alarm me. Campaigns have become more expensive to conduct, and the way campaigns are managed today has changed. One wag described the change this way: "Today a 'low-profile' campaign for local office calls for three public relations people, four media advisors, and five speech writers."

No, the problem is not just with the dollars. The

more serious problem is that the necessity to raise huge sums of money forces our representatives to participate in a process that detracts from their ability to serve us, and subjects them to great pressures and temptations from those who expect political favors in return for large contributions.

A few of the "receivees" have been indicted for succumbing to the temptations, and a few of these have been convicted of law violations. The Speaker of the U.S. House of Representatives, second in succession to become President of the United States, recently was forced from office, and the majority whip of that body met the same fate. The common denominator in both cases was money— essentially campaign money.

It seems to me that there is a Parkinson's Law, or perhaps a Monagan Law, which says campaign expenditures rise to meet campaign contributions. Or as Walter Zelman, Director of California Common Cause, has expressed it, "The campaign fund-raising and spending arms race remains in full swing." He went on to say, "Candidates prove their viability by arguing how much money they can raise."

It is even worse than that. In advance of elections, incumbents brag of raising huge war chests, in order to discourage others from opposing them, without regard to the actual amounts needed to win reelection. And all candidates raise money so they can convice hesitant contributors to join the bandwagon. This approach helps increase the flow of dollars.

With the style of modern campaigning, a strong argument can be made that ever larger contributions are needed to run a viable campaign. Television, radio, and direct mail are the primary mechanisms used in campaigns today, all of them very expensive.

It is also true that making a campaign contribution has become the only way that you can help the candidate or party of your choice. Previously, when campaigns were run differently, a person offering to help a candidate was offered a number of choices: he or she could staff a campaign office, address campaign material for mailing, call on households, hand out leaflets or bumper stickers, put up signs, and work in numerous ways to assist the candidate.

Now the response is simply, "send a check," and the devices for collecting these checks are very sophisticated. Money is funneled through a "political action committee" (PAC). PACs have been created by doctors, lawyers, teachers, labor unions, environmental organizations, corporations—and even nefarious individuals. Small contributions, collected this way, become large contributions. "Large" meaning they have more weight with the candidate.

This too, might not be all that alarming—what is alarming is that such war chests are raised at all, considering the lack of a valid need for them (at least, so far as the voter is concerned). Ninety-five percent of the incumbents are bound to be reelected, because they represent districts which have been reapportioned in such a way as to prevent a non-incumbent from winning the race.

Certainly not all money raised is spent on campaigns. One prominent assemblyman (who shall remain nameless) recently argued that it was proper to spend campaign-solicited funds for travel and other semi-personal uses—he happened to be one of the more ethical members of the legislature.

San Francisco Mayor Art Agnos, a former long-time member of the Assembly, was fined recently by the Fair Political Practice Commission for violations of the law and regulations. He paid the fine out of campaign funds. Nor is he the only person who has done this. Though not quite illegal, it certainly is very immoral to do so. The legislature quickly responded to the dilemma to make sure that it was legal.

It is most alarming that we can be solicited for campaign funds to pay for illegal activities. We even are seeing campaign funds being used to pay for the legal costs of legislators who have been charged with committing felonies. I am sure many contributors wish their money could be returned to them rather than used for these purposes. On the other hand, it bothers me that many other contributors (including most political action committees, corporate contributors, and some individuals) don't seem to care very much about these transgressions, or misuses of campaign funds. They choose to ignore the situation, and are quite prepared to contribute again to the same candidates.

Granted, this is not contrary to Napoleon Bonaparte's thoughts about the value of money, but the problem for representative government lies not so much in the *volume* of money, as *how* and *from whom* received. Representative government is destroyed when there is some *quid pro quo* with money and the manner in which our representatives vote.

There is a clear and increasing perception of this fact in the minds of the public. Rodney Dangerfield quips, "I get no respect. The way my luck is running, if I was a politician I'd be honest." A chasm, as wide as possible, needs to be in place to separate campaign contributions from when and where and how representatives carry out their responsibilities to their constituents.

Initiatives

"Republic—a government in which supreme power resides in a body of citizens entitled to vote and is exercised by elected officials and representatives responsible to them and governing according to law."
—*Webster's Collegiate Dictionary*

There is yet another major dilemma in the disappearance of representative government. That is the use and misuse of the initiative process. You can be sure that our forefathers, sweltering in Philadelphia in 1787, never thought for a moment about such a process as the initiative. They were powerful men in their own right, and were very carefully distributing power between the new federal government, state government, and the citizens.

They, in all likelihood, would have considered the great governmental experiment as doomed to failure if it required such a device as the initiative. No, the initiative is a modern invention, created to resolve abuses occurring in the representative process. It isn't historically fundamental to our unique system of representative government.

It would be disastrous if the people were to abandon the representative system, and yet recent widespread and unwise use of the initiative process offers uncomfortable evidence that they are doing exactly that. It is a foreboding development.

The use of the initiative has been expanded far beyond what was originally intended. The deterioration of the process is readily visible when one looks at how it is used today:

One. Addressing real issues that our representatives have failed to come to grips with in a timely manner. When one looks at the list of initiatives, in most cases this appears to be the least likely motivation, although it was considered to be the primary reason for introducing the initiative process.

Two. Addressing real issues which the legislature has dealt with in a way not to the liking of a minority or special interest group. This would be a proper use of the initiative if it weren't so easy to put initiatives on the ballot. If representative government is working satisfactorily, there should be few legislative actions that would justify taking the question to the direct vote of the electorate. Today, any well organized and financed group, even a small one, can challenge the decisions of our representatives and interrupt the orderly process of representative government.

Three. Addressing manufactured issues to make a profit. There is money to be made in the initiative process. W. C. Fields, of the bulbous nose but sharp wit, is credited with saying, "Take the money and run." His advice is being taken literally by those anxious to make a fast buck. A tremendous number of initiatives are proposed, regardless of whether they actually qualify for the ballot, or are approved or rejected by the voters, simply for profit.

Four. Raising issues for political advantage. Partisans in both parties now use initiatives as a political and campaign device. They are proposed to get the voters to examine opposition voting records or positions, or to stir the emotions and excite members of special interest groups so they will work hard to affect voter turnout.

Five. Embarrassing the opposition candidate or party. This usage is similar to the one above. Candidates for statewide office are using the initiative to advertise and exploit differences with their opponents. A carefully worded initiative can force a candidate to take a position that is sure to anger some voters. It is unimportant whether the initiative passes, or even qualifies for the ballot, as long as it upsets the opposition.

'JUST MORE POLITICAL CAMPAIGN MATERIAL, MRS. FENWICK.'

Cartoon courtesy Dennis Renault and the *Sacramento Bee*.

Six. Circumventing campaign spending laws. The latest distortion of the process serves as a way to raise more contributions and exceed current limitations on campaign spending. Since there are few restrictions upon the amounts that can be raised or spent on initiatives, this provides a sneaky way for candidates to evade the law.

These examples illustrate how something good can turn into something bad. Some people cynically suggest we should simply urge the voters to vote no on *all* propositions, theorizing that good initiatives will come back again. They don't explain how a so-called "good" initiative ever will pass if voters continue to follow their advice. But in any case, that just begs the question.

The long list of ballot proposals once had great value for incumbents at election time, and maybe it still does. It did for me. Before each election, I had cards printed with a list of the propositions and a place for people to mark yes or no. These cards, intended to be carried to the polls as a reminder of their choices, also included my name in prominent type!

During election seasons, service clubs, fraternal organizations, and other nonpartisan groups usually are reluctant to invite partisan candidates to speak to their clubs, not wanting to be accused of taking sides. However, many would invite me to come and discuss the long list of confusing ballot proposals as a *public service*. Naturally, I was happy to oblige, and I presented the pros and cons for each issue, without bias. If asked during the question period, I willingly expressed my opinions. It was an excellent campaign device for me at that time, and another example of the advantages enjoyed by an incumbent.

Fewer than half the states—23 to be exact—have a process like the California initiative in their constitutions or statutes. And, as usual, California is far ahead of the nation in the manner in which the use of this device has developed.

Much has changed since Hiram Johnson, the great reformer, gave us the initiative, referendum and recall rights in 1911. These were meant to be safeguards for the people to use whenever our government or our representatives got out of hand. It was designed to be used rarely, and then only when urgently needed, It certainly was not the idea of Mr. Johnson to substitute the initiative process for the officeholder. We still have elections to accomplish that.

Professor Betty Zisk of Boston University has written a book, *Money, Media, and the Grass Roots*, in which she examines ballot measure campaigns in California and three other states. In a recent presentation to the California Commission on Campaign Financing, of which I am a member,

Zisk discussed some of the motivations and end results of the Progressive movement to implement the initiative process in California.

She said the Progressive philosophy of the early 1900s sought to diminish special interest influence (the railroads in particular) over government. According to Zisk, the Progressives saw two key advantages in the initiative process:

> Policy-making powers would be given to the people, providing citizens with a more positive view of government. In turn, the voters would register and vote in higher numbers. The initiative process would create an additional check and balance system for the legislature ... [because] initiatives that were unsuccessful prompted the legislature to act on the issues they raised.

However, Professor Zisk went on to conclude that these two goals were not achieved. Instead of *countering* the power of special interests, as the Progressives desired, the initiative process actually has become another vehicle for special interest power. These groups merely adjusted their tactics to *use* the initiative process.

The use of the initiative today not only is outrageous, but is a dangerous course for us to follow as an alternative for representative government. Despite pretty strong evidence that our representatives have failed us repeatedly, use of the initiative is not our only recourse. We can stop electing them and elect other and better representatives (assuming we also reform the reapportionment process).

Eugene Lee, former director of the Institute of Governmental Studies, University of California at Berkeley, said recently that the initiative is becoming "the substitution of plebiscitary democracy for representative government." That substitution, Lee continued, "has left the state unable to address its basic needs in 1989, much less to face the challenges of the 21st century."

Richard P. Simpson, retired Executive Vice President of the California Taxpayers Association, who has had a long and successful career in the governmental arena, said of the initiative process:

> The notion that the initiative is some kind of grass roots safety valve to get around a special interest-dominated legislature is nonsense. It is becoming a self-perpetuating system in which the major winners are campaign consultants, lawyers, pollsters, signature-gatherers, computer mail specialists, electronic media and billboard companies.

Simpson concluded, "The major losers are frequently everyone in the state, except those specifically advantaged by a given proposal."

Most Californians do not understand that, once a constitutional initiative is approved by voters, the legislature is prevented from modifiying, changing, or adjusting the new law to meet new conditions or problems which arise. In the case of statutory initiatives, changes are possible, but the process is difficult.

The result is that changes require going back to the voters with another ballot proposal—and the length of the ballot list already is staggering, and increases with each election. The secretary of state informs us that there have been 1,024 statewide ballot propositions in the history of California, the first in 1884.

Assuming the current proliferation of initiatives continues, where it took a 112 years to reach 1,024, we will double that number in the next 21 years. If we truly believe in representative government, this is not the direction in which we should be going.

Many of the propositions are deliberately misleading, making it all the harder for voters to judge the merits of so many complex initiatives. There is an old gag that says, "no one is entirely useless; even the worst of us can serve as a horrible example." The following is a horrible example of what happens with propositions.

In the mid-sixties there was a movement among tax assessors aimed at taxing recreational properties on the basis of how they *could* be used, instead of their actual use. Taxing country clubs or private golf courses that were located in or near expanding commercial or industrial areas could have taxed them out of existence.

To correct this practice required a constitutional amendment, so a proposition for this purpose was placed on the ballot by the legislature. Passage was in doubt, however, and proponents feared that many voters would view this as a tax benefit exclusively for "rich" members of country clubs. Therefore, they persuaded the attorney general, whose job it is to give titles to all ballot propositions, to label it: TAXING GOLF COURSES.

The voters, reading the title and failing to examine the content, responded overwhelmingly in support of the measure. They supposed that by voting in favor they were *adding taxes* to these properties, when in fact the result was to *limit taxes*.

Misuse of the initiative is beginning to destroy many of our institutional elements. The most recent is the morass created by the passage of Proposition 103, dealing with insurance. As a former insurance agent who was involved with insurance legislation while a member of the legislature, I took time to study the five conflicting propositions dealing with insurance that shared the same ballot that year. Not one of them made sense.

Nor would I suggest that they did to many of the people who voted upon them. The voters imagined

'The first notice is from Ralph Nader saying my insurance premium will definitely be reduced; the second is from my insurance company saying it doesn't cover me anymore; the third is from the state insurance commissioner saying the company *will* cover me; the fourth is from the Legislature saying my premium cannot be raised; and the fifth is from the state Supreme Court saying it's a constitutional question.'

Cartoon courtesy Dennis Renault and the *Sacramento Bee*.

they could simply vote themselves auto insurance at reduced rates, but the economic world doesn't work like that. As a result, the insurance industry, whatever its faults, will be in a mess for a long time, and rather than benefiting, we consumers will pay a heavy price for this misuse of the initiative process. According to a *Sacramento Bee* story, insurance rates in that city are more likely to rise 15% to 25% than to be reduced because of the proposition.

It's not hard to guess what's in store for us if we persist in further misuse of the initiative process. I predict California voters will be confronted with a series of complex proposals addressing serious concerns about the delivery of health services. These initiatives will be (1) difficult to understand, (2) emotional in character, (3) confusing to vote upon, and (4) will not solve the problems in anything remotely related to a fair, efficient, or effective manner.

The group that gave us Proposition 103 is not through making changes. Advancing ever closer is another proposal that will surely diminish representative government's ability to work. It would *triple* business property taxes, under the guise of helping the individual property taxpayer.

Business might be able to pass some of that increase on to consumers—those very same property taxpayers—but it will make business less competitive, and thus hurt both consumers and current efforts to encourage job-producing activities in California. We will all be losers in the long run.

Putting initiatives on the ballot has become a new cottage industry. A whole new cadre of people and organizations is now available, equipped with the most modern computer mailing techniques. This new industry will *guarantee* the placing of an initiative on the ballot—for a price. Or given a sensitive and highly emotional issue—like lowering your taxes or insurance premiums, or protecting clean water—they will do it at *no cost* to the advocates, yet make a profit for themselves.

Other interest groups, many with large constituencies, can qualify initiatives themselves, without much additional help and with far less money. The newest of ideas in this context involves use of the so-called "christmas tree" approach. A group of organizations join together in support of a single initiative, such as the park bond measure on the June 1988 ballot. In this case, groups that raised money and/or gathered signatures on the petitions were rewarded by having their particular projects included in the bond issue—regardless of merit.

All of which served to eliminate representative government; our elected officials could not study, debate, or decide which of these developments should have had the highest priority or would best serve *all* the people of the state.

Dan Walters, a perceptive commentator on political and governmental subjects for the *Sacramento Bee,* characterized these initiative developments in this manner:

> Clearly, the degeneration of the legislative process into a systematicly corrupt and chronically unproductive morass has contributed to the phenomenon. People who have policy interests to pursue become frustrated with the Legislature's foot dragging and take their cases directly to the voters via initiatives.

And that is the rub. Substituting "plebiscitary democracy for representative government," as Gene Lee phrased it, is certainly the most dangerous threat to the precious and long-preserved system of government that the founding fathers provided for us. That carefully crafted system was not without detractors when it was first instituted. Time and trial has tempered it into one of the longest-running political shows in the history of the modern world.

Slowly that fragile system is being eroded, and the unwise and unintended use of the initiative process is aiding in the erosion. There are safeguards built in to our precious governmental system, and among them are the initiative, referendum, and recall. But that is what they are: safeguards. They are not supposed to be day-to-day functions or operations of government.

Unfortunately, barriers have been erected between us and the best safeguard of all: the ability to remove someone from office and replace that person with someone else of our choosing. These barriers must be removed. The following chapters deal with this problem and its solution. Once we have removed these obstacles we can solve problems in the way intended by our nation's founders, and we can reform and use the initiative process in the manner intended by Hiram Johnson and the Progressives of the 1910s.

Power to the Unelected

"We have relegated the ability to make compromises
to our staff."   —Senator Art Torres
                                             (Democrat, Los Angeles)

There is a compelling argument
that we no longer have representative government
when most activities are conducted by people who
never were elected to office. The introduction of
staff assistance for representatives has simply
raised one more barrier between us and our elected
representatives.

It is a modern—and dangerous—trend. It wasn't
until 1890 that the Congress agreed that each
representative should have a staff—of *one*. Even
as late as 1953, congressional staffs averaged at
two-and-a-half persons, including those who
worked in the home district. I happened to be a
member of such a staff at that time.

When I took office in the California legislature
in 1961, each of us was assigned one secretary in
Sacramento, who was available only when the legislature was in session. In addition, I was entitled
to a full-time secretary in my district office. In
those days they expected us to spend more time in
the district than at Sacramento.

Some observers of Congress claim its members began to lose touch with the people near the beginning of the twentieth century, in the first decade after staff members had been authorized. It seems to me that trend has speeded up dramatically.

Admittedly, our world and its problems (plus our increased awareness of those problems) have grown in complexity, greatly adding to the burdens of office. But with each gain in staff size there seems to be a corresponding loss in representative government.

Have you tried to contact your congressman or state legislator recently? Unless you're a personal friend or a major contributor, the chances of talking directly to your representative are practically nil. Which is not to say it's impossible, but you'll have to fight hard to break through the barriers created by staff.

This screening process is not without merit, for crank callers or salespersons shouldn't be allowed to waste the representative's time. But the flip side is that all too many staff people become imbued with their self-importance and want to make the decisions for the representative. Some, I suspect, have come to think of themselves as *the* representative. If your message does get passed along to the elected official, it will be in a "edited" form, often biased with the staffer's opinion.

Martin Smith, political editor for the *Sacramen-*

to Bee, said of former Assembly Speaker Jesse
Unruh:

> One of Unruh's important contributions was to sharp-
> ly improve legislative staffing so that it was no longer
> hamstrung by an overdependence on the executive
> branch and lobbyists for information and expertise in
> dealing with the state's problems. This improved
> staffing was a major reason that the California Legis-
> lature during Unruh's years as Assembly speaker
> became recognized as the nation's best body of state
> lawmakers.

The thrust of this idea from Unruh was one that I
supported. It was a very good idea to give the
legislature enough tools, so that they in turn were
not simply tools of the executive branch. Being
totally dependent upon the executive branch for
information and technical assistance put the legislative branch at a disadvantage.

The original concept was to have professional
staff members assigned only to the primary
committees, but the practice soon spread to every
committee. It was assumed these professionals
would be bipartisan, and their assistance would be
available equally to all legislators.

When I followed Unruh as Speaker in 1969, I
continued this policy without change. It was a
mistake on my part. I believed that committees
should employ experts who remained on the staff

regardless of which party or persons were in power. This would permit the development of a continuous knowledge base that would be available to a changing team of legislators on each committee. But I soon discovered that not all professional staff people were, or wanted to be, bipartisan. It would have been better if I had been selective.

Martin Smith took note of this development in his story about Unruh, writing:

> The legislative staffing system, which was intended to help lawmakers effectively explore questions of public policy, has become more of a political support apparatus for the party caucuses and individual lawmakers seeking to become power brokers.

In my year as Speaker of the Assembly, the budget for the legislature was just under $24 million. (I remember how hard we labored to arrive at that amount; we didn't want the media to report it as $24 million—somehow a figure like 23.9 had a better ring to it.) Although it is hard to obtain precise numbers (for they are jealously guarded by the legislature), the current budget is about $200 million. The overall budget has increased by $127 million in just the last ten years.

This staggering increase did not occur because we pay the legislators that much more money. As a matter of fact, legislative salaries have increased very little during this time. No, the increase is nearly all attributable to the increase in legislative staffing. The number of staffers has grown from 700 to 3000 in this period. The list of positions and numbers is staggering: clerks, secretaries, interns, administrative assistants, district office personnel, committee professionals, consultants, researchers, and a whole host of others.

Their actual duties include professional legislative services, campaign fundraising, and campaign direction. These positions provide on-the-job training for young people who plan to run for public office, and in many cases amount to out-and-out political patronage.

The average salary for all staffers is about $27,000, and it can exceed $100,000 for some—a lot more than the governor receives. Compare that with what we pay the people we elect to represent us in Sacramento: their current salary is $40,816.

On top of that, the legislature has recently instituted a "bonus" system to provide additional compensation for high level staffers. There may be justification for higher pay based on merit, but there is no justification for a bonus system. Of course, it's possible the public might support a bonus system based upon the ability of staffers to reduce the cost of running the legislature!

There may be something to the old adage that many a promising young man has been ruined, or reduced to mediocrity by getting his hands on too much power before he was able to handle it. The problem once again is not so much with the people involved, for it is likely we can assume they are hard working and dedicated. But the system is faulty, and I suspect that one third, and probably more, could be lopped from the payroll without damage—at least no alarming damage—to the legislative process.

Of course, that isn't the central theme of this document, which is to demonstrate the effect of excess staff upon representative government.

Another Smith, Hedrick, said in his book, *The Power Game*:

> Government has become so complex and the top leaders so daunted by its complexity that they have granted enormous powers to staff aids who labor in the shadows.

His book was directed at the federal government, but it applies equally to our state legislature. California legislative staffers are not quite as direct and powerful as those in the Congress, but they are catching up rapidly.

This dangerous situation is further confirmed by a prominent Washington lobbist, James Lake. Lake is a former Californian, and an experienced national Capitol representative for many of our state's interests. Lake is quoted as saying in the February issue of *California Business*, "On all but a very few issues, it's the staff people who determine positions."

A primary concern of mine is the amount of time these staff people devote, at taxpayers' expense, to direct and indirect political campaigning. Some of these activities are highly visible, but innumerable functions are performed that are not easily identified, but whose whole intent is to contribute to the next election of the boss.

A second and equally disturbing result of excess staff is the incredible increase in the number of bills introduced at each new session of the legislature. It is a quite natural result, when you consider that every enterprising staff person assumes it is his or her role to come up with proposals for new laws. Most staffers are young, idealistic, fresh out of school, and simply bursting with ideas. More ideas than can be considered, in fact.

The third concern of mine is that staff members are being "promoted" to the legislatures. With increasing frequency, being a staffer has become the inside track to winning a seat as representative. A great number of young people, after deciding to seek political office, sign up as staff members in order to achieve this goal. Because of what has happened to the election process, it often works.

We have an actual case of one elected legislator whose only previous experience consisted of serving on the staff of another legislator, whose only previous experience likewise was limited to time served on the staff of a third legislator—three generations of inbreeding.

Now, please understand; this is not meant as an attack upon any of these people, who in general are bright, able, and have some experience. But they have missed out on the real world of constituents and community. They hardly qualify as "citizen" representatives of their districts.

On October 8, 1989, *Sacramento Bee* reporter James Richardson quoted State Senator Art Torres during a discussion of how a certain critical legislative issue had been decided. According to Richardson, Torres said, "We have relegated the ability to make compromises to our staff." Perhaps I do a disservice to Senator Torres by highlighting his words at the beginning of this chapter. I may have quoted him out of context—but his words precisely describe what is happening to representative government.

Compromise is the central core of representative government. We resolve issues, which necessarily involve many divergent views and interests, with "give and take"—in a word, *compromise*. It is not a dirty word. In the foreword to her *Miracle at Philadelphia*, Catherine Drinker Bowen wrote:

Compromise can be an ugly word, signifying a pact

with the devil, a chipping off of the best to suit the worst. Yet in the Constitutional convention the spirit of compromise reigned in grace and glory; as Washington presided, it sat on his shoulder like the dove.

Compromise is the cinch pin of representative government. The ability to compromise is the eminent power that we entrust to our elected representatives. When we allow it to be delegated to the unelected, we lose a basic element of democracy.

A certain amount of staffing is absolutely necessary. Our representatives could not do their jobs otherwise. The danger is overstaffing and over-influencing—and most of all, the substitution of staff people for the individuals we have elected. When staff acts *for* the representative, with no accountability to the electorate, we have arrived at a greatly diminished version of "representative" government.

Regulation Without Representation

"It is hard enough to keep government pure when only a few industries were regulated. . . . But in future, if virtually all economic life is drawn into the governmental web, who will be left to defend the interests of the general public?"   --Paul Howard Douglas

$\mathbf{W}$e have all heard the expression, "When the going gets tough, the tough get going," but in the case of our representatives, it seems not to have been the case. When the going got really tough, our representatives didn't get going at all. Instead, they created new regulatory agencies to take the heat and manage the problems.

This was not quite what the early creators of representative government had in mind. They jealously guarded against infringement upon their prerogatives to legislate matters. It is unimaginable that they would surrender power to a secondary level of government. It seems not to have been part of the thinking of the constitutional framers.

It was a long time in our history before the Congress willingly gave up any of its powers. Society had to become more complex, issues more controversial, problems more difficult, before that could occur. Eventually Congress threw in the towel. "Give the ball to someone else," might have been the refrain. It must have looked like an easy way out.

Hence the creation of powerful regulatory agencies like the Interstate Commerce Commission and the Securities and Exchange Commission. The die was cast. Proliferation began. First Congress, and then state legislatures took up the practice. At the beginning only one or two, but soon dozens, then hundreds—finally thousands—of powers we had entrusted to elected representatives were shifted off to secondary players—the regulators.

Only they weren't secondary for very long. Over the years they have managed to become primary players in the governmental process. There is logic for some regulatory bodies. They can and do serve an important role, and probably contribute a service that could not (or would not) be provided otherwise.

"Protection for the public" often is the covering blanket to justify creation of these agencies. This excuse serves to distract attention from another purpose: to shift responsibility for controversial decisions away from our representatives and onto the agencies. Even when there is an acceptable reason to create an agency, we must not forget that the regulatory process is an *interference* with representative government—a substitution for it.

Abuses common to the regulatory process include self-expansion of powers, arbitrary decisions without voter examination, and self-perpetuation. (Who ever heard of a regulatory agency going out of business?) And, although such agencies can free up the time of our representatives, a tremendous amount of legislative staff time is spent dealing with regulatory agencies on behalf of constituents. Why? Because there is no straight or easy route the public can use to intervene with regulators. As regulatory agencies are created there seems to be a commensurate need for increased legislative staff.

Oddly, the fact that this works to the public's disadvantage turns out to be a tremendous asset for alert legislators. Every time the representative can resolve or smooth over a constituent's problem with a regulatory agency, that action translates into support at election time. Computer files scrupulously remember these "favors." Invitations to fund-raisers are sent in a timely manner—just before the next election.

Maybe—just maybe—there is nothing nefarious about all this. But is it mere coincidence that so much of the hot water into which our representatives tumble comes from the quid pro quo of regulatory contacts and campaign contributions? Senator Alan Cranston's difficulties with savings and loan industry regulators provide a clear example of the pitfall that exists when our representatives intervene with regulators on behalf of their constituents and/or contributors.

Equally serious is the problem caused when people of intelligence and good intentions agree to serve on regulatory bodies, and then fall into what I think of as the "tender trap." The problem is not simply that they will regulate our lives—though they will, unrepresented though we may be—but that they will *overregulate* our lives. It is a rare occurrence for a regulatory body to underregulate on an issue or problem.

A problem is tossed in their laps. It is controversial. Information is lacking. What new developments will occur in the future that will make today's decision seem to be wrong? Let's say you are a commissioner with the Food and Drug Administration, and a new drug is presented to you for approval. All kinds of tests and evidence about the efficacy of the drug and its safety are presented to you. Thousands of tests have been conducted on animals and humans. It appears to be safe, but should you approve it?

Ten years later new evidence may come to light that the drug has many problems. Would you risk the possibility that some people will say that it was your fault for approving it? Like most of us, your tendency would be to bend over backwards—to *overregulate* its use.

A recent conversation with Dr. Paul J. Feldstein, Professor at the Graduate School of Management, University of California at Irvine, reinforced that thought. Feldstein has written a book called *The Politics of Health Legislation*, and we talked about how one balances the thousands of lives that might be saved by use of a drug against the possibility that a few lives might be lost because of some presently unknown side effect. If the probabilities are that thousands will benefit immediately if it is approved, is it correct to wait for more information that may disclose some negative evidence that might cost the lives of a few?

We concluded that, the human equation being what it is, the tendency would be to overregulate its use and protect yourself, even though thousands of people might die because of this overly cautious approach.

Cyclamates! Now there is a great example of regulatory powers running amuck. Earlier in this book I mentioned Jack Veneman, who served in the Assembly with me. Later, when he was Under-Secretary of Health, Education, and Welfare, Jack was involved directly in one of these regulatory fiascos. In 1970 we spent a summer holiday weekend with the Venemans, at Rehoboth Beach on the Delaware coast. His next-door beach-neighbors, the noted political commentator Bob Novak and his wife, were also there. Novak was not quite as noted then as he is today, and we were all frolicking in the waters of the Atlantic when Veneman received an urgent call from his boss, Bob Finch. Finch was Secretary of Health, Education, and Welfare, as the department was structured then.

Finch had received urgent phone calls from his office and from the White House about a report being released by the Food and Drug Administration. A study showed some mice had died after consuming a quantity of soft drinks containing cyclamates.

Because cyclamates were being used as a sugar substitute in many foods, panic broke out—the press as usual helping to create the panic. Consumer groups joined the outcry, predicting doomsday consequences if prompt action wasn't taken to ban the substance. Meanwhile, anguished screams were heard from food producers, who described the severe economic loss they would suffer if the cyclamates were banned.

The use of cyclamates was stopped, even though the study was not conclusive about the deleterious nature of cyclamates. Millions of dollars in sales were lost, and millions more were expended to find an acceptable substitute. The result? Sixteen years later further research clearly showed there was no danger from cyclamates unless you were a mouse who could imbibe sixteen bottles of an artificially sweetened soft drink at a single meal.

Not only are we victims of the overregulation syndrome, but improvements in technology have actually worsened the situation. It was common, not too many years ago, for science to measure and report things in *parts per thousand*. This jumped quickly to *parts per million*, and now it is parts per *billion*. This ability to measure, for example, a potential cancer-causing agent in parts per billion of some product, or some other staggering number, has helped to create scares in the public mind. It has also exacerbated the idea that we can produce an absolutely safe society.

The public has nearly forgotten one very recent official scare, caused when some agricultural inspectors found two, repeat *two*, cyanide-spotted grapes in a shipment from another country. The regulators sprang to action, the media jumped to news breaks on television and giant headlines in newspapers and magazines, and screaming messiahs joined the hue and cry, to save us from this deathly threat. It cost millions of dollars to our economy (and that of the producing nation) before the flap ended, almost before it had started.

Overregulation! It is a costly adventure in non-representative government. How many products and other items and buildings now display that great comment, "This may be hazardous to your health?" One day soon, given the direction we're heading to achieve a fail-safe society, we'll probably require doctors, when delivering a baby, to stamp the rear end of each new child with a permanent notice stating that "Living is dangerous to your health."

It really is nearly that bad. In every public place are signs to warn us about something that might cause us untold damage. Incidentally, nobody pays any attention to them. One person went into a restaurant recently, and the waitress said to him, "I am required by law to tell you that everything you have ordered may be harmful to your health."

Two Northwestern University professors gained instant fame when they published a study correlating hospital mortality rates with stringency of state regulation. Steve Shortell and Edward Hughes, in an article published by the *New England Journal of Medicine*, concluded that states with strict expense rate controls had mortality rates about 6% higher than the least-regulated states.

I was involved in what has become one of the more difficult developments in the area of regulation. I was Speaker of the Assembly when the environmental movement—I'm really not sure what a "movement" is—began to be an issue in the legislature. Legislators either were personally interested in the subject, or they had begun to feel the heat from environmentalists to do something about protecting our environment.

There was a parallel political eruption at the

time involving the campus disturbances. Governor Ronald Reagan called them "open rebellion," while others referred to them as the "free speech" movement. At any rate, the campuses, the legislature, and the public were about evenly divided between offering sympathy or sending in the National Guard to suppress the revolution.

To come to legislative grips with these two extremely sensitive and divisive issues, I tried a new departure in committee structure. While I was a congressional assistant, I became aware of the use of "select" committees to deal with single subjects. The idea was to examine the problem, report back to the legislative body with recommendations, and then abolish the select committee. Normal standing committees then would review the proposed legislation.

I appointed a Select Committee on Environment. It was uniquely composed of chairmen from the various standing committees that had some responsibility for portions of the environmental problem. Assemblyman Jack Knox, the chairman of the Local Government Committee, was the logical choice to chair the select committee.

Others appointed were George Milias, chairman of the Natural Resources and Conservation Committee; Pete Wilson (now a U.S. Senator), chairman of the Urban Affairs and Housing Committee; Carley Porter, chairman of the Water

Committee; Bill Ketchum, chairman of the Agriculture Committee; and Gordon Duffy, chairman of the Health and Welfare Committee.

The report that they rendered to the legislature was thoughtful, comprehensive, and controversial. More Democrats than Republicans were sympathetic, which posed internal political problems for me as a Republican Speaker who was attempting to get votes for those legislative recommendations.

In context with this discussion about regulation, one of the committee's controversial recommendations was that there should be an examination of potential environmental problems whenever projects were undertaken, and a report of the results should be published. The legislature at this time understood "projects" to mean construction or demolition projects.

This recommendation became the greatly applauded California Environmental Quality Act. The widely damned Environmental Impact Statement (EIS) was a key part of it. This legislation was narrowly passed by the legislature, after assurances were given that this meant only that potential or real environmental problems would be *looked* at before a project was undertaken. The act, by itself, would not be a reason or device for stopping a project—it was a way of discovering potential problems, which if found could then be addressed.

Implementation of the law began, regulations

were drafted, disputes developed over proposed projects, and before long there were challenges in the courts. Environmentalists succeeded in obtaining specific interpretations of the law never intended by the legislature. Some lower courts decided projects could be halted or terminated if an EIS showed any environmental problems.

When this view was challenged, Jack Knox, himself a strong environmentalist, argued against the broader interpretation. He provided the California Supreme Court with records of his committee and the debate to show "legislative intent." Despite this evidence, the court concluded otherwise.

Based upon the court's decision, regulators proceeded to expand upon the EIS criteria. Recently, a Sacramento Superior Court judge cancelled the black bear hunting season because the State Fish and Game Commission hadn't considered environmental impacts of the annual hunt. This is a far cry from what the legislature had intended. It serves as an example of how well-meant regulation can go astray, and why overregulation serves to diminish representative government.

Someone who admired George Washington and enjoyed the numerous legends about him, lately observed that it was a wonder to him how anybody could cut down a cherry tree without first filing an environmental impact report. Our nation's history might be different if this regulation had been in effect. Washington would have a "criminal" record that opponents could have used against him—the story would have appeared on page one of the local gazette! Negative public reaction might have caused Washington to drop out of the Presidential contest.

Methodist Bishop Ernest A. Fitzgerald of Atlanta, Georgia, wrote:

> Centuries ago an itinerant tentmaker wrote a letter that is still being read today. In that letter, St. Paul wrote, "whatever you sow, you will also reap." Sometimes that sentence is taken as a threat. It really isn't. Rather, it is a description of the way things work. There is a dependability in creation which requires a seed to reproduce its own kind.

There is a relationship between the bishop's comments and how our representatives go about creating new regulatory agencies. When a problem arises that they have trouble dealing with, our legislators plant a regulatory seed which begins to "reproduce its own kind." Though they are responsible to the people, these representatives now believe they can ignore the growth of the regulatory function, because they no longer see it as their *direct* responsibility—one more example of how representative government is disappearing.

Impact of Modern Media

"If we can take the media and lawyers in America—and I speak for all CEOs—and move them to Japan, the U.S. could be competitive in 24 hours."
—Ross Johnson, CEO, RJR Nabisco.

The growth and changing character of the media, especially television, has put a whole new dimension into politics and government. At the time of our founding fathers, newspapers and some other print media were the primary means of communicating to the public. It was not instantaneous, but the news could be absorbed in a leisurely fashion.

In a 1988 article for *American Heritage*, Greg Mitchell wrote:

Today's television commercials make and break candidates, and campaign coverage by the media has a significant impact on public opinion. Substance sometimes appears to count for little, and image for almost everything. It is little wonder that image makers, not experts on the issues, now dominate campaign staffs.

Larry Collins, former publisher of the Pasadena

Times Star, commented that the print media also had gone through dramatic changes in its relationship to politics and governance. In early days, California newspapers had been influential participants in the political process. Collins recalled that at one time there had been as many as 26 independent publishers in the Los Angeles area. Each was personally interested in the selection and subsequent performance of the representatives from his area.

These publishers exercised political power and influence in the communities served by their newspapers. Their editorials were read and heeded by many of their subscribers. It mattered to them who represented their communities, and they followed closely the activities of those representatives. They had influence (too much, some would say) over those representatives.

They had good reason to be interested, because publishers lived in the communities served by their papers. A publisher lived in, invested in, and profited from the prosperity of that local community. He had reason to care.

Now those independent publishers of newspapers have almost all disappeared—chains and conglomerates have scooped them up. The moguls who own and control today's newspapers are absentee owners, interested chiefly in the profit and loss statement. Their interest in the local community, and thus who represents it, is often negligible.

At one time, the *Los Angeles Times* was a powerful influence in California politics. Severe critics have said the *Times* was the "political dictator" of that era. It may have been true. The owners of the *Times* were immensely concerned about what happened in their community, and about the nature and character of the people who represented them.

The editorial support of the *Times* was important—often essential—to congressmen, senators and assemblymen. It wasn't too long ago that *Times* reporters in Sacramento would circulate on the Assembly floor to let Los Angeles area representatives know how the *Times* felt about certain issues, and less than subtly suggest how each should vote. That was a period when rules were a little looser about allowing access to the floors of both houses. Also, in those days before one-man one-vote, Los Angeles County had but one senator to inform.

Newspapers had an impact, no question about it. By contrast, present-day editorial support for individual candidates has very limited influence on local races, and only slightly more impact on statewide races or ballot propositions. This is true of the *Times* and of most other newspapers that are controlled by absentee owners and imported publishers.

This development, plus the emergence of television and the ten-second "sound bite" have nearly eliminated the influence of newspapers in the area of representative government. If the officeholder or office seeker has the right kind of voice and ability to exploit the ten-second limitation, he or she has a chance to grab attention on television news programs. But with that kind of reporting we aren't apt to hear much of the truth or even a complete story. If a candidate lacks such a "voice," or the local newspaper is disinterested, how can the message reach the public?

Former Governor Jerry Brown learned how to exploit televison's standard news format with great skill. He understood that if you wished to appear on the 6 o'clock news, you had to prepare a statement that was attention-getting and catchy—and say it on camera in ten seconds or less.

Think about that. Try to say something intelligent about a complex or controversial subject in that time frame. You can't do it. But the political image makers, and skillful people like Jerry Brown, can exploit this method to their advantage.

Unfortunately, it does not contribute to better public understanding of issues. It amounts to misinformation. And this can be fatal to the democratic process.

Most political races in California are conducted primarily with television commercials, contrived "news" aimed at the 6 o'clock news, and direct mail. The latter has taken on a new dimension, thanks to the magic of the computer. Computer analysis of voter profiles has provided a new, and *totally biased* way of reaching the electorate. The success of modern direct mail techniques has made newspapers even less necessary to political campaigners. Newspapers are reduced to reporting successes, failures, and scandals.

This translates into a situation where politicians hunt for headlines instead of solutions. It's government's obligation to make sure that its citizens receive honest information; it's not government's role to invent or conjure up information. That may not be entirely original, but it decidedly states what the practice ought to be.

When George Washington gave his farewell address in 1796 he commented, "In proportion as the structures of a government gives force to public opinion, it is essential that public opinion be enlightened."

It's not always the media's fault that we don't receive honest information—we get what we pay for. After all, newspapers, magazines, and television are in business to make money (although it seems to me there was a time when they felt their prime responsibility was to inform and educate the public). They make a living by agitating people, and if people become sufficiently agitated, their representatives will take notice.

An extreme example of this is the recent flap over an ABC "news" broadcast. Even ABC admitted its misjudgment in not labeling a news "simulation" as what it was: a staged reenactment of a spy investigation.

It comes as no surprise that results of a recent survey conducted by the *Times Mirror* Center for the People and the Press indicate the American public believes there is political bias in news coverage. Newspapers fared better than television in this survey. But it should startle everyone that 49% of the respondents thought news organizations fueled controversies by their coverage, while only 46% thought they merely reported the news.

Incumbent politicians possess unlimited opportunities to exploit the modern media. They have the ability to grab attention and to make their voices heard. No one seems able to compel them to tell the whole story. In this they are abetted by the media, which requires brevity and thus encourages our representatives to tell less than the truth. The media, in a sense, have become makers of the news. The ten-second blurb, contrived news, investigative reporters, and editorializing news commentators have served to distort the activities of representatives in government.

Someone has written, "When the Roman Empire was falling apart, the people were kept busy with the circus. Now we have television."

Our representatives are being encouraged to become performers rather than persuaders. Some (not all) of the floor discussions in the U.S. House of Representatives are conducted in front of television cameras. The calm debaters and point makers are rarely seen on camera. Or perhaps the calm debaters and point makers change into performers when the camera points in their direction. The camera's red light has such a hypnotic attraction for legislators that the California Assembly is preparing to admit live television to its chambers.

It really would be revealing if live, unscheduled, and roving cameras focused on the members' non-attendance at committee meetings, or showed lobbyists buttonholing legislators in the halls of the Capitol. How about filming the antics of those representatives who think the media isn't watching? Naturally, I don't advocate this, but it is a thought.

The private lives of early representatives (especially some who drafted the Constitution), wouldn't pass the scrutiny of today's press. And their conflicts of interest were considerable, even then. That, of course, does not make the illegal or immoral actions of today's representatives defensible. It only shows that the people we elect won't be too different from the society that elects them, if they're truly representative.

The ability to manipulate the media by some,

means there are other voices that won't be heard. Or that their messages may be misunderstood, because they lack the skill to *use* media. There must be a place in the system where people of good will, differing backgrounds, and representing a wide variety of constituents and interests, can have a free and open exchange of ideas. The public needs access to such people and their ideas in order to reach the artful compromises essential to our form of government.

And here it is only proper to mention that when the framers of the Constitution were drafting the most significant document in our history, they met in *secret*. On May 25, 1787, when enough of the delegates finally gathered in Philadelphia to create a quorum, they closed the doors of the chamber in which they were meeting. The media of that day never saw the inside of the hall when the delegates were in session.

In fact, the public never knew exactly what took place until years later. The momentous debate, labored discussion, vitriolic diatribe, and historic compromises were accomplished in absolute secrecy. We only know of these matters because 35-year-old James Madison took copious (and unauthorized) notes of the proceedings. He is said to have positioned himself in the front row of the room for that particular purpose. All the delegates

SPEAKING OF SECRET SESSIONS

Cartoon courtesy of Dennis Renault and the *Sacramento Bee*.

were sworn to silence, and very few of the now common "leaks" came from these public officials.

Americans didn't find out that George Washington had presided over the convention until much later. One could speculate that it might have been common information in the local pubs, but the media reported little of what was happening. They had no direct access to the deliberations, nor speedy means of getting the news into print. Without Madison's effort we would have no record at all of this historic event. His notes were not even published until 1836.

Today it is hard to disagree with the premise that all public business should be conducted in public, or to say the media shouldn't be privy to these actions. They are the mechanism through which people learn of the deeds and deliberations of our representatives.

Perhaps there is a way the "open meeting" laws could be amended to provide our representatives with an opportunity to *deliberate* over significant issues—without taking secret ballots—in the same manner that our Constitution was created. I'm sure that if those delegates had been concerned with getting ten-second "sound bites" on the six o'clock news, we wouldn't have our remarkable Constitution.

It is imperative that we have a free press. Nothing in this book is meant to indicate anything to the contrary. My whole purpose is to show how far we have wandered from that goal, and why we must improve the process. Many public representatives manipulate the media, and the media has helped perpetuate the practice by helping such persons stay in office.

The quiet but critical debate is lightly reported in the print media, and hardly at all on television. The actions of rambunctious, sign-waving demonstrators on the Capitol steps are reported by the print media as a minor event, and as major news in the visual media. Many representatives become more interested in what is reported, and how they are perceived, than in the solving of problems. And if the media doesn't actually create these people, it certainly does advance their careers.

Fortunately, there are many thoughtful and concerned members of the media. One of the more respected and insightful persons in that profession is David S. Broder. Broder, currently political columnist for the *Washington Post*, is a long time observer and commentator on the American political scene.

In a January 4, 1990 column in the *Post* he wrote about "Our Strangling Democracy." Expressing great personal concern, Broder stressed the responsibility that the press has in seeking a "renewal for democracy." Broder wrote:

> We cannot allow the 1990 elections to be another exercise in public disillusionment and political cynicism. Three elements are crucial—and in each, the press has a significant role to play.

I was favorably impressed by the fact that Broder's three elements parallel the concerns expressed in this book. It is encouraging that a highly reputable member of the media should be writing in this vein about the press's responsibilities. Not many members of the fourth estate are so forthright.

Thomas Jefferson, in a letter written to George Washington in 1792, said, "No government ought to be without censors; and where the press is free, no one ever will. If virtuous, it need not fear the fair operation of attack and defense. Nature has given to man no other means of sifting out the truth, either in religion, law or politics."

Conclusions and Recommendations

"There is nothing more difficult to take in hand, more perilous to conduct, or more uncertain in its success than to take the lead in a new order of things."
—Niccolo Machiavelli

In early days in our country it was the custom on the Fourth of July to hold a big celebration in the city park. The local band would play, the minister would give the invocation, and the principal speaker would be called upon for the address. He would not necessarily be the best orator in town, but he would be the one with the loudest voice—there were no public address systems in those days.

More often than not, the speaker would shout "We have reached the crossroads" of whatever was the crucial problem of the day. Of course, now we would have to shout "We have reached the cloverleaf!" Nonetheless, we *have* reached a dramatic point in our history concerning our political process. It is time today for some new shouting and oratory in the parks and on the platforms.

The Great Seal of the United States bears the motto *novus ordo seclorum*, meaning "a new order of the ages." That certainly is needed now in our governmental process. I hope I can convince you that we must make immediate and significant changes if we are to recover, restore, and reinforce representative government. If we don't act quickly, I think it's not overly pessimistic to say we may lose the opportunity forever.

It's time once again for the people to take things into their own hands. Only the electorate can decide this fundamental question. This is not a putdown of our present representatives—simply an acceptance of the facts. It's humanly impossible for them to deal with these questions in a disinterested manner. Any reasonable solution will necessarily be very painful for current officeholders.

Politicians simply cannot come to grips with the necessity to restore representative government. Some of my best friends are politicians, but few are statesmen. "A statesman is a dead politician." This often repeated quote sounds like the remark of a disillusioned cynic, but it was said by Thomas Reed, a former Speaker of the U.S. House of Representatives.

It will require many great acts of statesmanship to reform our system, and I suspect few legislators are willing to die politically in order to become living statesmen. If we are to accomplish any important reforms, the voters must do it.

It is *their right* to establish the ground rules for our representative government. It's also their right to decide how reapportionment should be conducted, what the terms of office should be, how long and how often the state legislature should be in session, and how much we are willing to pay our representatives.

On the other hand, it's properly within the province of the legislature to determine the day-to-day conduct and functioning of the legislative process, as long as they conform to the ground rules laid down by the people. The people have an appropriate right to dictate policy to the legislature. It would not serve any appropriate cause to dictate the procedures used to deliberate those policies.

I lost a few Republican friends when I sided with Assembly Speaker Willie Brown against a ballot proposition that would have diminished the powers of the Speaker. It would have restricted the manner in which the legislature conducts its day-to-day business. I didn't defend the current Speaker's *use* of those powers, of which I disapproved, but I argued the right of the legislature to determine its own modus operandi. (I also argued that the proposition was unconstitutional, a contention later confirmed by the state supreme court.)

The Assembly must provide the Speaker with strong powers over the functioning of that body. It is the only way to get 79 strong-willed people to reach the artful compromises which are the hallmark of the legislative process.

So it all comes down to the people.

We cannot address questions relating to the federal government without changing the U.S. Constitution, and that is a very cumbersome process. There is no right of initiative, referendum, or recall in the federal Constitution. The only way to bypass the officeholders is to use the initiative process, so we must start in California. If we can succeed here, it may spread to the national level. If we are indeed the bellweather state, perhaps our influence will be felt throughout the nation, and eventually in Washington, D.C.

So how do we start? It's Utopian (and foolish) to imagine we can remake the whole system until it is pristine. We don't live in a perfect society, and imperfect voters won't elect perfect representatives. Congress and the state legislatures are a reflection of us.

My approach is Machiavellian: Reforms should be simple to understand, simple to enforce, and interrelated. We need sufficient and workable reforms that will meet as many of our objectives as possible. My list of areas in need of reform would include (1) reapportionment, (2) legislative operations, (3) campaign financing, and (4) the initiative process.

Some of the reforms I'll describe aren't new.

I'm reminded of the newly-hired minister who delivered his first sermon and received many compliments about it from the congregation. Because of their warm reception, the pastor decided to give the sermon a second time, which resulted in some grumbles about the repetition. But when he gave the same sermon on the third Sunday, the congregation was extremely angry. When they complained to the minister, he replied, "Yes, you've heard the sermon before—but nobody is practicing the message!"

Solution One

The most important reform to be addressed concerns reapportionment. If we could alter only one process, our first priority should be to make changes in how we draw up our districts—how we allocate seats in the legislature. One way or another, we *must* change the existing process. It is the bedrock issue. But I hope we can do more. To do a thorough job and address as many problems as possible, we shouldn't stop until reforms in all four areas have been enacted. They work like dominoes, one upon the other.

A number of proposals have been made that

would improve the reapportionment process, and some have a fair chance of being approved by the voters. But I'd like to suggest another approach, that goes a step beyond the others. In 1968 I introduced a constitutional amendment in the Assembly that would have caused the number of state senators to be the same as the number of the congressmen in California, and would have pegged the number of assemblymen at twice that number.

There was little support for the idea then, so perhaps I was premature. Let me offer a few reasons why I think its worth serious consideration.

Our state representative districts contain too many voters at the present time. California's population grows rapidly every year, but the number of districts has remained constant since 1861. After nearly 130 years, the inevitable result is that each district contains more people than can be effectively served by its representatives. In 1861 the state had 4,749 constituents per assemblyman, and about 9,499 for each state senator. Today each member of the Assembly represents more that 350,000 people, and senators have twice that many constituents.

In 1861 the entire state of California contained 379,944 persons, who were represented by 34 senators and 80 assemblymen! One doesn't have to be a mathematical genius to see that the ratio of representatives to constituents has increased astronomically. There's little doubt that a modest increase in the number of state legislators would be beneficial.

For these statistics I am indebted to Don A. Allen, Sr., who represented the 63rd Assembly District in Los Angeles County until 1966. It was Allen who pestered the leadership every session he was in the Assembly, persisting until they agreed to continue publication of the *Legislative Sourcebook*, a most valuable compendium of information on legislative history. Unfortunately, it is no longer published. Fortunately, my library contains an old copy. It helps greatly to have this history to put current questions in proper perspective.

(Allen, a crusty, ex-Marine, who also served a stint on the Los Angeles City Council, once became somewhat exasperated during a prolonged debate over a long series of criminal justice bills. Finally, he asked for the floor and announced: "We should stop spending time on these bills until we get the people to start obeying the Ten Commandments.")

Where would we put these new lawmakers? A modest, and easily accomplished reduction in the legislative staff—perhaps one third—would solve this problem. It would also have a salutary effect on that other problem: overstaffing. The present Senate and Assembly chambers could easily be reconfigured to accommodate this small increase.

How small? If the reapportionment law were enacted soon, the increase in the legislative size would be determined by the number of members of Congress to which the state is entitled in 1993. The federal Constitution requires that after each decennial federal census, the number of congressional representatives in each state will be determined by reallocation of the 415 members of the U.S. House of Representatives according to the new population figures.

California now is allotted 45 members—the anticipated population increase will raise that number to about 50–52. If we assume 52 (the likely number), that would result in 52 state senators and 104 members of the Assembly. There is nothing alarming about such an increase (we now have 40 and 80 respectively), and it would decrease the number of constituents for each legislator to represent.

But this doesn't resolve the main business I talked about earlier—the unfair drawing of district boundaries. Here is where the "Machiavellian" part comes in!

In 1991, following the 1990 census, under my reform plan the California Supreme Court would appoint a "Master." The Master would not draw a plan, but he (or she) would solicit and review plans which could be submitted by anyone—political parties, organizations, ordinary citizens, and even the state legislature could participate.

The Master would conduct extensive public hearings and would examine each plan to determine if it met the basic criteria spelled out in the reform act. What would I include in the list of criteria? Here are my suggestions:

1. There will be as many congressional districts as are allocated to the state, an equal number of state senate districts, and twice that number of assembly districts.

2. The congressional and senate districts shall be coterminous, and each senate district shall be divided into two assembly districts. The four State Board of Equalization districts will be comprised of as many contiguous state senate districts, or a portion thereof, as would make them equal in population.

3. The districts will conform in population, to be constitutional in character, thus meeting equal population requirements.

4. Each district shall provide fair and effective representation for all our citizens, including racial, ethnic, and language minorities.

5. Districts shall be drawn to minimize division of geographic regions, cities, counties, and other easily recognizable political subdivisions. Counties with a population greater than a new district shall first be divided into whole districts, and only the remaining population used to form part of another district.

6. Districts will be composed of whole census tracts.

7. New districts shall be consecutively numbered, north to south, and where possible, state senate districts with the greatest percentage of population from concurrently even-numbered districts shall be given even numbers, and odd numbers given to those districts with greatest percentage from currently odd-numbered districts, except when necessary to deviate from this rule to ensure an equal number of even and odd numbered districts.

Other criteria could be mentioned, but already there are enough counterbalancing influences in these suggestions to meet the basic objectives.

After examining each plan and determining if it did or did not meet the requirements, the Master would recommend *one* plan to the California Supreme Court, for the court's approval and implementation. No modifications could be made to the plan as submitted.

I am in favor of giving the legislature first shot at the process. To permit this, I would suggest that any plan which had received a two-thirds vote in both houses of the legislature and been approved by the governor would be reviewed first. It would be submitted to the Supreme Court, along with the Master's opinion that it did or did not conform to the criteria. If the Court determined that it met the requirements, the plan would become effective.

If the Court found the legislative plan did not conform, it would advise the legislature what changes would be required. If the legislature made the changes, the plan would be resubmitted and go through the same procedure.

If the legislative plan is not approved, and cannot be altered to meet the Court's objections, the Master then will submit to the Court whatever plan, submitted from any source, that most accurately meets the criteria outlined.

Most other plans for revised reapportionment take the authority completely out of the hands of the legislators. This probably is the way it will be accomplished, but my plan at least provides an opportunity for the legislature to reapportion in conformity with the people's wishes. Some perhaps will accuse me of still having some residue of legislative blood in my veins.

Whether the legislature would care to accept the challenge is doubtful at best. First, there is the requirement to obtain a two thirds vote of both houses—hard to do when currently even a resolution designating Mother's Day would receive a bare majority from the present legislature.

Second, it requires the governor's signature. No matter who is governor at the time, this won't be easy. Republicans hope the chief executive will belong to their party, feeling this will work to their advantage in the reapportionment process. However, it didn't work that way in 1971, when the Democrats controlled both houses of the legislature, and Ronald Reagan was governor.

There is almost no question that the Democrats will control both houses again when 1991 rolls around. Only a handful of Republicans still cling to the hope that they can gain control of one house by then. That doesn't seem realistic to the others, whose chief hope is that a Republican will occupy the governor's chair.

Democrats also would like to see their candidate win, but they know it's not important in terms of reapportionment. They believe, with historical support, that enough Republicans will be anxious to obtain a "safe" district, that it will be no trick to obtain the necessary two-thirds vote to override *any* governor's veto.

I would really like to be around to watch the legislature wrestle with reapportionment under the provisions I've just outlined. Having observed and/or participated in the reapportionments of 1951, 1961, 1971, and 1981, I can hardly wait for 1991, especially if played under a new set of rules.

Can you imagine the internal battles? Which member of Congress would want to see what senator, who would want to see what assemblypersons, all corraled in the same area? Who would be most suspicious of whom? Who would be waiting in the political weeds to take them on in the next election? Oh, there would be a lot of bloodletting!

With 7 new congressional districts, 12 new senate districts, and 24 new assembly districts, I can visualize the battle now: Republicans versus Democrats, urban versus rural, north versus south, Black versus Hispanic, liberal versus conservative. The Battle of Gettysburg would look like a Sunday school picnic, compared to that!

My plan has a lot to recommend it: It will decrease the number of constituents per district. It will ease the pain of dealing with incumbents. It will offer better opportunities for Hispanics and Asians to be represented. It will make it possible to draw lines that will encompass fast growing areas of the state, without harshly impacting other areas that might lose representation.

It will make more districts, and will make all districts more competitive. It will encourage better candidates, some of whom will resemble the citizen representatives we used to have. That is what it's all about.

Solution Two

Without solving reapportionment, nothing else will be enough. At the same time, solving the reapportionment problem alone is not enough. We need to make a few changes in the legislative arena also. Most important is the need to limit the length of legislative sessions.

I say this as one who stood firmly on the other side of this issue in the past. James Russell Lowell said, "The devil loves nothing better than the intolerance of reformers." So I imagine some of my legislative friends—assuming I have any left by now—would consider me somewhat intolerant.

It is a fact that I was a vociferous participant in past efforts to give the legislature greater flexibility in the matter of legislative sessions. I feel sometimes like the defendant who stood before the bench and asked, "Judge, may I plead slightly guilty?"

Some do not remember that it wasn't very long ago that the legislature met for six-month sessions in odd-numbered years, and held 90 day budget sessions in the even-numbered years. That was the system when I was elected to the legislature in 1960. I helped change the system. There were excellent reasons for the changes that were made. The present basicly unlimited two-year session is appropriate in theory.

There are now excellent reasons for revision, for the theory has become distorted in practice. Cynics would say the chief reason for the extra length is to provide legislators with more per diems. As I wrote earlier, that was not my reason for supporting the lengthened sessions, nor is the matter of compensation a reason for my changed position. Whatever we decide to pay legislators, we must reduce the session time for different reasons.

To put it simply, the legislature should adjourn each year on July l. Period!

If I supposed there was a danger the legislature couldn't complete the state's business by midyear, I wouldn't impose this arbitrary deadline. But there is absolutely no reason why it can't be done. If today's legislature can't do it, it's because we have the wrong people representing us.

I am not persuaded that 120 very bright and able legislators, supported by 3000 staff people, with a $200 million operating budget, can't finish their work by July 1. I guess this calls for another Monagan Law: "The business of the legislature will consume whatever time is allotted."

It is true that there are many problems in a state the size of California. The issues are stickier and more difficult to confront than they once were, but they won't get any simpler as time passes. Sticky, difficult, and controversial though they may be, problems need to be confronted in a timely manner, and not postponed. It's not the size of the workload that produces log jams in the final days of a session—it's procrastination that does it. Another Monagan Law says it all: "Tough decisions are delayed until the last possible minute."

The crucible of a deadline is necessary to resolve the politically gut-rending issues. There are other advantages, too. It will help restore more representative government by bringing the legislators back home, where they will have a chance to become "citizen" representatives again.

It would cut the cost of running the legislature. It would reduce the need for large staffs. Fewer lobbyists would be hired (there goes the lobbyist vote). There would be less time to hold fund raising affairs in Sacramento (back comes the lobbyist vote). The last is an issue that can be handled with another reform, but the July 1 deadline will help this problem as well.

When emergency issues arise, and the legislature is not in session, there has to be a mechanism for the legislature to reconvene. One reason for changing to a biennial session in 1966 was that the Constitution permitted only the governor to reconvene the legislature in "extraordinary" sessions. He could call for a session whenever he chose, and the legislature was required to consider only what the governor placed on the agenda.

In 1964 Governor Pat Brown called the legislature into five separate and different extraordinary sessions. The files and bills for each session had to be printed in a different color of ink, and it was almost comical to see the kaleidoscope of colors the bills and files produced on one's legislative desk. But the problems were more than just color confusion; the conflict was legislative versus executive power.

The need to maintain the independence of the legislative from the executive branch is important, and the constitutional changes made in 1966 gave the legislature the right to call itself back into session. There needs to be such a provision, but it should be reserved for those rare occasions when a governor is unwilling to reconvene the legislature, and then only when there is strong indication the legislature will respond to the emergency in a prompt and expeditious manner.

Such a procedure might require that a petition to reconvene be signed by a majority of the members in both houses, which would be a clear sign the issues to be considered are of major concern. A deadline for adjournment of the urgency session should also be required.

Many people are concerned about the number of bills, resolutions, and constitutional amendments that are introduced in a single legislative session. There are too many, and half are unnecessary. But we shouldn't restrict the right of our representatives to introduce them, for that isn't the problem.

The legislative leadership manages the process after the bills are introduced. What happens to the bills from this point on is the problem. Rules are violated, bills are heard over and over again (but never killed), hearings are delayed, measures resurrected and amended, and dozens—in some cases hundreds—of bills are replicas of each other.

This is careless, wasteful, and unnecessary. All kinds of procedures are available to handle these problems, and legislative leaders are well aware of them. If the sessions were shorter, wise leadership would be forced to stop these harmful practices. There is nothing in the Constitution, and at the present, nothing in the rules, that says a measure has to be heard simply because it has been introduced. All measures could be given prompt and expedited courtesy, and meet the July 1 deadline.

Appropriate compensation for legislators is a very controversial subject. Witness the heavy flak when the Congress tried to raise its pay. When this was attempted in 1988 it generated so much heat that congressmen backed away from the issue. In 1989, the outcry wasn't as bad, but the action didn't go unnoticed. In an editorial cartoon in the *San Francisco Chronicle* on November 19, 1989, a character labeled Congress tells Uncle Sam:

I've run up a trillion dollar debt on your account. I've bilked you for $300 billion more in savings and load fraud, I exempt myself from laws that I make and you must obey, I'm involved in endless scandals of corruption and deceit. You deserve better. Restitution must be paid—punishment must be meted out. I'll start by giving myself a raise.

Most people who see this cartoon will conclude that Congress shouldn't get a pay raise. But the fault isn't with the pay raise—the fault is with the people we elect. That's where the change should occur.

It is hard to define what is appropriate compensation for elected officials. They aren't employees in the traditional sense. They are volunteers, not draftees, and since they are not supposed to be life-time employees, but on contract from election to election, we need some different criteria to determine the right amount of compensation.

Then as representatives, reflective of society itself, we can't judge and pay them on value received. Some of those we elect would be worth three times more than others; some would be judged to be worth very little. The public impression sometimes is that they aren't worth anything. Under the best of circumstances, most voters will resist the idea of raising their salaries. If there was a proposal on the ballot to cut legislative pay in half, it likely would be defeated because the cut wasn't big enough.

If we are to restore the idea of citizen representatives, and we ask people to interrupt their existing careers, separate themselves from their families, run through the abuse of campaigns, and subject themselves to the rigors of public life, it is only fair to offer acceptable compensation in return.

Staff members in many instances are paid twice as much as legislators. Constitutional officers, cabinet secretaries, department heads, and a whole myriad of state officials are compensated considerably more than legislators.

As part of my package of reform in the areas of reapportionment, campaign financing, and shortened legislative sessions, I would propose also that we pay legislators the same as municipal court judges, which today is about $86,000. If they aren't worth that much, don't elect them.

When I talk about this to public groups, you can hear the groans when the $86,000 figure is suggested. However, when I say, "Hold it a minute, I am recommending this increase as a reward for spending less time in session," the groans turn to cheers.

But if we raise the pay to some level like this and eliminate (1) the excessive payment of per diems, (2) perquisites that substitute for pay,

(3) honoraria paid that are near-bribes, because of the manner in which they are given and received, and (4) the transfer of campaign funds to uses that are substitutes for compensation, we will have a much more honest and appropriate approach to compensation.

For it is a fair level of compensation if we take away several devices that have been substituted for compensation, and if we put more of these representatives in competitive districts where their jobs are at greater risk.

First I would take away the misuse of per diems paid to legislators when they are in session or engaged in legislative business. It is terrible in fact, and awful in perception, when the legislature keeps itself in session, often with no better reason than to collect their per diems. I'm sure to get a laugh when I propose paying them when they're *not* in session, rather than when they are. Per diem abuses obviously contribute to this reaction.

I suggest that we pay them the same per diem paid to other state employees, when the legislature is in regular session. They should receive this only for the days when they are actually in attendance at the session. The practice of "recessing" over the weekends so per diems will not be interrupted is neither savory nor defensible.

When the legislature is not in session, but legislators are on legislative business, they should be entitled to claim reimbursement for expenses. They would file a claim, stating the reason and that it was for legislative business, and sign it under penalty of perjury. Which recalls another infamous quote from Jesse Unruh. He used to say (and I've heard him say it), when asked to approve a claim for reimbursement of some legislator's expenses, "If you've got guts enough to submit it, I've got guts enough to sign it."

With disclosure of all outside income (which would be limited to 15% of legislative compensation, and unrelated to legislative responsibilities), elimination of honoraria, limitation of per diems, and no transfer of campaign funds for personal use, they will deserve the compensation that has been suggested. The taxpayers will be money ahead—you can count on it!

Should we limit the number of terms a person can serve in state government? That's another issue that surely will be on the ballot soon. We seem to get considerable turnover among the constitutional offices, such as governor, lieutenant governor, et al, without any restrictions. No governor has held the office for more than two terms since Earl Warren in the 1950s.

A persuasive argument can be made that a limit should be placed on the number of terms served by legislators. I've entertained the thought myself in the past, but I've changed my mind. To begin with, if we believe in representative government, we should have the right to elect whomever we please, and thus for as long as we please.

The people did go along with the constitutional amendment to limit the President to two terms, and that is probably all any President could stand in these days. It also is consistent with the precedent set by our first President, George Washington, who refused a third term, although he could have served for life had he wanted to.

As usual, my track record is somewhat ambivalent on the subject. I wrote earlier in this book that I switched parties from Democrat to Republican because I didn't believe Franklin Roosevelt should run for a fourth term. Now I'm convinced we should go no further than the presidency in limiting terms.

I suspect the current interest in limiting terms is a misguided reaction to problems created by unfair reapportionment. We can solve these problems better by redrawing district lines to encourage competition. Competitive districts really do impact on longevity in office.

Solution Three

The third major issue needing revision is the question of campaign financing. I am a member of the California Commission on Campaign Financing, an auspicious group representing an excellent cross section of California society. Assisted by an outstanding staff, this commission conducted an extensive study of campaign financing in California that was the basis for Proposition 68.

That proposition was a detailed restructuring of the laws governing campaign contributions and expenditures, and it sought to introduce tight control over the process. Proposition 68 included an element of public financing in order to meet court tests concerning the limitation of campaign expenditures. I am strongly opposed to public financing of campaigns, and I agreed to support the report and the initiative measure only after the commission agreed to my proposal to prohibit transfer of funds between candidates. This was accomplished in a spirit of compromise.

But despite the passage of Proposition 68, Proposition 73, and later rulings by the Fair Political Practices Commission and the courts, we appear to have deeper problems and more abuses than ever before. Propositions 68 and 73 were both well intended, yet they have driven us into a new morass. Better answers are needed.

Of the several new proposals to re-cleanse the political campaign finance system that have been announced so far, all suffer from the same difficulty as the earlier plans: they attempt to solve every

'YOUR HONOR, THE SENATOR REQUESTS A BRIEF RECESS IN HIS TRIAL ON CHARGES OF ALLEGED BRIBERY AND EXTORTION SO THAT HE CAN VOTE ON LEGISLATION CRUCIAL TO SEVERAL IMPORTANT CAMPAIGN CONTRIBUTORS.'

Cartoon courtesy of Dennis Renault and the *Sacramento Bee*.

143

conceivable abuse that can be imagined, with the result that they are confusing and conflicting. The result, as now, will be less compliance and less penalizing of violators.

To avoid this pitfall, my own proposals are few in number, simple to understand, and easy to police. They do not cover every possible abuse that might occur—but they will control about 95% of the ugliest and least ethical elements of present-day campaign practices. They are three in number:

One. No one shall solicit, promise, receive, or otherwise arrange for a campaign contribution until such time as the candidate has officially filed for the office sought.

Two. Contributions shall be expended only during the election for which they were solicited; i.e., they cannot be transferred to another candidate, or used for any other purpose than for campaign expenditures for that election.

Three. Any surplus remaining in the campaign fund 30 days after the election shall be transferred to the State Treasury General Fund.

The penalty for violations by representatives should be very severe—such as forfeiture of office. There is a constitutional precedent for this penalty. I can testify to that because of an experience I once had. In the mid-sixties, while serving as the minority leader in the Assembly, I received a phone call from Dick Barkle, a former college roommate who then was head of public relations for Pan American Airways.

He invited my wife and me to be guests of the airline aboard Pan Am's inaugural flight from New York to Frankfurt, Germany. It was to be a VIP trip, and naturally I accepted, elated at the invitation and the honor it inferred. I hung up the phone and returned to the floor of the Assembly, where I informed my friend Bob Beverly (an assemblyman then and presently a state senator) of the exciting news.

To my surprise, Beverly casually asked if I really wanted to do that. Then he proceeded to remind me of the potential consequences of taking the trip. Bob was a lawyer, and a little sharper on constitutional matters than I was at the time. He referred me to Article XII, Section 7 of the California Constitution, which reads:

> A transportation company may not grant free passes or discounts to anyone holding an office in this state; and the acceptance of a pass or discount by a public officer shall work a forfeiture of that office.

But for the prompt advice from my friend, that might have meant the abrupt end of my service in the legislature. The penalty in the constitution was meant to be harsh in the instance of free transportation. It goes back to the days when the railroads dominated the legislative scene, and this was a way for the reformers to retaliate.

It's a penalty that could easily be applied to present day violations by elected representatives. The threat of that penalty would get stronger attention and better compliance than "slap on the wrist" fines.

So there you have it: three simple steps. That really is all that needs to be done, and while it won't make the system perfect or pristine, it will eliminate most of the unsavory aspects of what is happening. It might even help lessen the cynical truth of the words written by Thomas Fuller: "They that buy an office must sell something." Of course, Fuller was writing about the Civil War and Reconstruction period.

No single change by itself will accomplish what is necessary to restore representative government, but when we combine these rules for campaign financing with a fair reapportionment scheme, and reform in the legislative process, the various proposals will work together to get the job done.

We've got to attack all these problems at one time. We can't afford to follow the example of the country whose leaders wanted to change from the British style of driving on the left side of the road, but were unsure how to proceed. Unfortunately, they decided to phase the old system out.

Solution Four

If only dealing with the initiative process were as simple as the first three I've discussed. No politician in his or her right mind would suggest today that we ought to do away with this option for the people. On the other hand, nearly every responsible person now recognizes how much it has been abused in recent years. It has become a draconian usurpation of representative government. *The initiative is a "safeguard," not a "vanguard."*

The California Commission of Campaign Financing and other groups are seriously examining the problems with the initiative process. Although 23 states have the initiative prerogative (27 don't), none of the others so far have experienced California's problems. Examination of how it works in other states may help us find an acceptable answer. But meanwhile, it seems nearly impossible to find a cure that won't destroy the patient.

For example, raising the number of signatures needed would increase the difficulty and/or expense of qualifying initiatives. But this would be a large obstacle to the citizenry-at-large, for whose benefit the process was created. It would have minimal impact on the activities of professional or special interest groups, whose resources could more readily accomodate the changes.

The present requirements, as outlined in the State Constitution, Article II, Sec. 8 (6), are not burdensome as it relates to the number of signatures required to qualify an initiative. The present volume of those initiatives making it to the ballot should provide at least prima facie evidence to the conclusion that it is too easy to qualify initiatives.

Presently the Constitution requires signatures to equal 5% (for statutory initiatives) or 8% (for constitutional amendments) of the votes cast for all gubernatorial candidates in the last general election.

Rather than increase the number of signatures required for qualification, I would like to see some sort of review process before they are placed on the ballot. I propose that the Secretary of State be required to transmit any initiative measure that had qualified for the statewide ballot to the legislature for a review.

If proponents of the initiative preferred to avoid this review process, they could do so by obtaining twice the number of signatures otherwise required for qualification. This would represent a modest increase—10% for statutory initiatives and 16% for constitutional amendments. This in itself would have a salutory effect by diminishing the number of initiatives lacking widespread support.

The review process could consist of three steps:

One. The legislature would be required to hold public hearings on initiatives that have otherwise qualified, before they could be placed on the ballot. The legislature could not delay the proposals or alter their language, but would provide a public opportunity for both proponents and opponents to debate the issue before the onslaught of distorted campaign material hits the tube, radio, and mailbox. If it wished, the legislature could take a recommendation vote on the issue, to help guide public information.

Two. The attorney general and the legislative counsel would be required to testify to the legislature about the constitutionality of the initiative, and other legal experts might also be called, or otherwise given the opportunity to testify.

Three. The legislative analyst would be required to testify about any fiscal implications. While it is true that some of this information is included with the ballot pamphlets sent to voters, I doubt that 20% of the voters read any part of it, or that 1% read it cover to cover. I wouldn't even venture a guess about how much is understood of the material that is read.

Even those who write the pro and con arguments in the ballot pamphlet are not held to any test for veracity. In fact, in many instances the authors hardly address the subject of the initiative. The legislative public hearing would at least give both sides a chance to challenge their opponents head to head.

It is even possible (however unlikely it now appears) that the legislature might then be encouraged to pass acceptable legislation of its own to mitigate the problem addressed by the initiative. It wouldn't knock the initiative off the ballot (unless the proposers agreed), but such action certainly would help crystalize the issue for voters.

The End Result

Action on all four of these proposals would get us back on the road to good and *representative* government: (1) a public interest reapportionment process; (2) assisting in the return of our legislators to citizen representative status; (3) some enforceable campaign finance restrictions; and (4) minor revisions in use of the initiative.

That would do it.

Naturally, there will be those that will argue against these proposals. Some will say they don't go far enough. I would agree that there is more, much more that could and perhaps should be changed some day. But I'm convinced that any attempt to correct *every* fraility in this somewhat fragile governmental system is doomed to failure.

Others I suppose will look upon these proposals

as very revolutionary, but they're not. They're as new as our problems, and as old as our Constitution. As I said at the outset, "This book is about *representative government*." That may have been a revolutionary proposal in Philadelphia in 1787, but not in California in the 1990s.

My object has been to discover solutions that are possible of achievement, simple to understand, and will do the job. It is equally important that they should be easy to implement and enforce. These suggested changes do just that.

U.S. Supreme Court Justice Louis Brandeis said: "To secure respect for law, we must make the law respectable."

We must indeed.

Epilogue

"I am going to speak my mind because I have nothing
to lose."   —S.I. Hayakawa

A journalism teacher was
once asked by a student, "What are the principal
ingredients in writing a successful book?" The
teacher said the book should contain references to
four essential elements: deity, royalty, sex, and
mystery. The next day, the student came to class
and announced that he'd written a book. His book
was, " 'My God,' cried the Queen. 'I'm pregnant,
who did it?' "

As you have noticed, none of these elements are
in this book, nor will they appear in this epilogue.
Nevertheless, I hope what I've written about my
personal experiences in government and politics
will give some credibility to my conclusions. As I
said at the beginning of this book, my recommendations are political, but not partisan. They are
honest, because I have nothing personal to gain by
suggesting them.

Epilogue

I'm speaking my mind because although I really
have nothing personal to lose or to gain, we as a
state and a nation have a lot to lose, and much to
gain by making a few modest improvements in our
governmental system. That's why I've chosen to
write this book, not about people or politicians or
some abstract feature, but about our ability to
resolve differences and achieve economic and
societal well-being. More important, it's about
restoring public trust in our political system,
founded in Philadelphia in 1787, and nurtured for
over two centuries.

An editorial in the *Los Angeles Times* of May
28, 1989, struck at the heart of what all the debate,
dialogue, and discourse is about. Entitled "Restore
the Public Trust," it said:

> The problem with the American political system today
> may not be that it is so corrupt, but that it is so
> corrupting. Powerful, intelligent and trusted political
> figures who should know better are on the take. The
> public trust cannot be upheld on Mondays, Wednes-
> days, and Fridays. Political corruption is as old as
> political history. Perhaps the dividing line is blurred
> these days. Reform laws seek to correct past abuses,
> only to introduce loopholes that attract new abuses.
> The solution is to remove temptation entirely. Or
> make it absolutely clear what is allowed, and what is
> not allowed. Make the punishment simple, swift, and
> severe. If the people want a restored public trust, they
> must be willing to pay for it.

Restoring public trust and confidence in their representatives is what it is all about.

If there is doubt in anyone's mind about public perception of politicians in this state, the California Poll released in August 1989 should remove it. The California Poll is conducted by Mervin Field, who has been so closely associated with polling opinions in this state for so long, and is so highly regarded, that many people refer to "the Field Poll." The *San Francisco Chronicle* headlined its report of the August 1989 results of this poll, "Public Doesn't Trust State's Politicians."

So what else is new? The poll showed that, by a 2–1 ratio, people believe state and local politicians are less honest today than they were 10 to 15 years ago (I'm glad I was a politician in that earlier era). The poll results revealed that 42% of the respondents felt today's politicians are less honest and ethical than they were a dozen years ago or so. And 73% said there was no difference in these characteristics between Democrats and Republicans.

The first startling point I'd like to make about this poll is not so much the poor opinion of politicians generally, which was to be expected, but the fact that public perception of their elected representatives has *worsened*. The second significant point is that the public, despite such feelings, has done nothing about it. If there is such widespread disillusionment among the people, we should be doing something to remedy that situation.

If our representatives—most of whom are honest, dedicated, and sincere—are perceived as dishonest and sleazy, something serious has gone wrong. It's not completely impossible for our representatives to undertake the task of revising the system. But few would be willing to risk their public careers to do it. Unlike the rest of us, they have much to lose.

If our representatives are unable or unwilling to set it right, then "we, the people," as the preamble to the Constitution puts it, must undertake the restoration of the public trust. We, the people, must rise to the occasion.

As strongly as I deplore the practice of substituting the initiative for the legislative process, at least it will provide Californians with an avenue for action. We have to break the logjam somehow, and this appears to be the best tool at hand.

This can't be done at the federal level, so the best we can hope for is that our success will encourage other states, and eventually the Congress to follow our example.

As governor of California, Ronald Reagan was fond of saying he was trying to start a "prairie fire" that would philosophically sweep the nation. Whether he was successful, history will have to determine, but the concept did propel him into the presidency. We, the people of California, have the opportunity to meet an important challenge that, who knows, may ignite a prairie fire that will sweep the nation, and restore genuine representative government everywhere in the country.

Lest anyone think that the citizens of California cannot make these suggested changes, let's examine the state constitution: Article II, Section 1, states, "All political power is inherent in the people. Government is instituted for their protection, security, and benefit, and *they have the right to alter or reform it when the public good may require.*" (My emphasis.) It's now time to do exactly that!

"The deterioration of every government begins almost always by the decay of the principles on which it was founded." We would do well to heed these words of Baron de Montesquieu. It's time to reestablish some of the *principles* upon which this country and its unique form of government were founded.

This country was not built on elitism. Quite the contrary—deciding who would represent us was not based upon the idea we would seek out and then hire the best and brightest in the land. Representation means society should be reflected in the legislatures. The premise is that men then, and men and women now, should be people who live in and understand the community—and the community should know them. The premise is that the position is not to be occupied in perpetuity by a career politician. It should be expected that people would serve at some personal sacrifice, and not seek (or require) the office as a vocation.

Our reforms must be designed to reinforce these principles, and aim to achieve the essential goal of "citizen" representation. If we are to succeed in any reform effort, the thread of this principle must be woven tightly into the fabric of each new law. Aristotle wrote, "It is better for a city to be governed by a good man than even by good laws." But we must have good laws to help the good men be good.

What we need are a few laws, and a few regulations, that help ethical people function in that manner in our government and political system. As the *Los Angeles Times* editorial stated, "Make it absolutely clear what is allowed and what is not allowed. Make the punishment simple, swift, and severe."

I suppose you could say this is a Paul Revere-ish book, written to "spread the alarm." Not everyone appreciates being informed of troubling matters, and I know there were some who disagreed with Paul's activities and those of his Boston patriot friends. Even now his role is not always appreciated. The story is told of a Boston salesman who was visiting a client in Texas. The Texan boasted at great length about how the heroes of the Alamo held off whole armies, unaided, and then sneered:

"I don't believe you ever had anyone brave come from Boston."

"Didn't you ever hear of Paul Revere?" asked the Bostonian.

"Paul Revere?" retorted the Texan. "Oh, yes. Isn't he the one who ran for help?"

Help! That's what we need. How many of us will take up arms to save our representative government?

President George Bush said, "Standing up, speaking out and fighting for what is right is the true meaning of responsible citizenship. It is the ultimate power of democracy."

The same thought was expressed over 150 years ago by the French jurist and political historian, Montesquieu. In 1748 he wrote, "The tyranny of a prince in an oligarchy is not so dangerous to the public welfare as the apathy of a citizen in a democracy."

The head of a large firm was asked what it took to reach the top. "The same thing it took to get started," he responded. *"A sense of urgency about getting things done."*

We know what needs to be done. We have the means to accomplish it. We need the will to do it.

It is urgent that we start now!

Monagan's Laws

Campaign expenditures rise to meet
campaign contributions.

The Republic cannot successfully survive with
alienation of those who serve from those who elect.

Government by the regulatory process does not
provide the best result, just the average result.

Our democracy is unique; it has survived because it
is representative with safeguards. Unfortunately,
the safeguards are taking over.

Majority decisions are not always right, unless an
inordinate amount of time and resources are used
to inform the public.

There is a direct mathematical relationship between
the number of legislative staff and the number of
bills introduced.

All representatives are bad—except mine.

Legislation is accomplished by compromise; that is settling differences by mutual concessions. Unfortunately, many constituents feel that compromise is an act of treason.

There is no such thing as underregulating. By nature of the process, regulators will only overregulate.

In politics, luck is better than skill anytime.

The business of the legislature will consume whatever time there is for it.

The tough legislative decisions are delayed until the last possible minute—or forever, if possible.

The initiative is a safeguard, not a vanguard.

A. Proposed Constitutional Amendment To Change the Method of Redistricting

Existing provisions of the California Constitution provide for a Senate of 40 members and an Assembly of 80 members and require the legislature to adjust the boundary lines of the Senate, Assembly, United States House of Representatives, and Board of Equalization districts in the year following the federal decennial census, according to prescribed standards.

This measure would repeal these provisions. It would instead provide for a Senate equal in size to the congressional delegation, and for an Assembly of twice that size.

This measure would specify the requirements redistricting plans would be required to meet. The measure would require the California Supreme Court, in the year following the federal decennial census, to appoint a Special Master, and would require the Special Master to review any plan submitted by the California legislature by the first day of July following completion of the federal decennial census, approved by a 2/3 vote of the membership of each house, and approved by the governor.

It would require that the plan be submitted to the

court along with the opinion of the Special Master that the plan does or does not conform to specified requirements. If the court determines that the plan conforms to the requirements, the plan would become operative.

If the legislature did not submit a plan, or the plan did not conform to the requirements, the Special Master, after public hearings, would be required to recommend a redistricting plan meeting the requirements received from any political party, organization, or citizen, or if none were submitted, one recommended by the Special Master.

AN AMENDMENT TO THE CALIFORNIA STATE CONSTITUTION RELATING TO REDISTRICTING

There is proposed to the people of the State of California that the Constitution of the State be amended as follows:

First—That subdivision (a) of Section 2 of Article IV thereof is amended to read:

SEC. 2. (a) The Senate has a membership ~~of 40 Senators~~ *equal to the number of members of Congress apportioned to California pursuant to federal law,* elected for 4-year terms, ~~20~~ *one-half, or as nearly as possible,* to begin every 2 years. The Assembly has a membership *equal to twice the number of Senators* ~~of 80 members~~, elected for 2-year terms. Their terms shall commence on the first Monday in December next following their election.

Second—That Article XXI thereof is repealed.

Third—That Article XXI is added thereto, to read:

Amendment A

SECTION 1. Redistricting of the Senate, Assembly, Board of Equalization, and United States House of Representatives shall be governed by this article.

SEC. 2. Any redistricting plan adopted pursuant to this article shall provide for all of the following:

(a) As many congressional districts as are apportioned to the state, an equal number of Senate districts, and twice that number of Assembly districts.

(b) Coterminous congressional and Senate districts which consist of two Assembly districts.

(c) Four Board of Equalization districts comprised of as many contiguous Senate districts, or a portion of one thereof, necessary to make them equal in population.

(d) Districts which are as equal in population as is practicable.

(e) Districts which recognize fair and effective representation for all citizens of the state, including racial, ethnic, and language minorities.

(f) Districts drawn to minimize division of geographic regions, cities, counties, and other easily recognizable political subdivisions. Counties with a population greater than an entire district shall first be divided into whole districts and the remainder of the population shall form part of another district.

(g) Districts which are composed of whole census tracts.

(h) Consecutively numbered districts, north to south and, where possible, even numbers for senatorial districts with the greatest percentage of population from currently even-numbered districts, and odd numbers for those districts with the greatest percentage of population from currently odd-numbered districts.

Amendment A

SEC. 3. In the year following the year in which the decennial census is taken under the direction of Congress, the Supreme Court shall appoint a Special Master for purposes of this article.

SEC. 4. (a) If a redistricting plan which is approved by a vote of two-thirds of the membership of each house and approved by the Governor is submitted to the Special Master by the first day of July in the year following the year in which the federal decennial census is taken, the Special Master shall review the plan for conformity with the requirements of Section 2. The plan shall be submitted to the court along with the opinion of the Special Master whether the plan conforms to the requirements. If the court determines that the plan conforms to the requirements, the plan shall become operative.

(b) If the court determines that the redistricting plan submitted pursuant to subdivision (a) does not conform to the requirements of Section 2, it shall advise the Legislature on the changes needed to make the plan conform. If, within 30 days of receiving notice from the court, the Legislature and Governor adopt an amended plan in the same manner as the original plan, and the court approves the amended plan, the amended plan shall become operative.

SEC. 5. If no redistricting plan becomes operative pursuant to Section 4, the Special Master shall recommend to the court another plan submitted by any political party, organization, or citizen which the Special Master determines conforms to the requirements of Section 2 for the court's approval and implementation.

SEC. 6. The Special Master shall conduct public hearings prior to making any determination and submitting any redistricting plan to the court pursuant to Section 4 or prior to recommending any plan to the court pursuant to Section 5.

B. Proposed Constitutional Amendment Relating to Legislative Sessions, Salary, and Expenses

Existing provisions of the California Constitution provide that terms of members of the legislature commence on the first Monday in December next following their election.

Existing provisions of the California Constitution require the legislature to convene in regular session at noon on the first Monday in December of each even-numbered year. Each regular session adjourns sine die by operation of the Constitution on November 30 of the following even-numbered year.

This measure would require the legislature to recess on or before the first Friday in July of the odd-numbered year, to reconvene on the first Monday of the even-numbered year, and to recess before the first Friday in July of each even-numbered year, except the legislature would be authorized to reconvene the regular session to legislate only on specified subjects.

Existing provisions of the California Constitution require the compensation of members of the legislature, and their travel and living expenses, to be prescribed by statute, as specified.

This measure would repeal these provisions. It

would require the annual salary of a Member to be the same as the annual salary of a judge of the municipal court. The measure would authorize Members to receive payments for travel and living expenses, as specified, at the same rates paid to other state officers and employees.

Existing provisions of the California Constitution require the legislature to enact laws prohibiting members of the legislature from engaging in activities or having interests which conflict with the proper discharge of their duties and responsibilities.

This measure would prohibit a Member from soliciting or receiving, and a person from offering or giving to a Member, any honorarium, gift, or other payment that has any relationship to a Member's duties and responsibilities as a Member of the Legislature.

Existing provisions of the Constitution provide that any bill presented to the governor that is not returned within 12 days becomes a statute, except the governor has until September 30 of the second calendar year of a session to act on bills passed by the legislature before September 1 and in possession of the governor on or after September 1 of that year.

This measure would provide instead that any bill not returned within 12 days becomes a statute, except the governor would have until July 31 of each year to act on bills passed by the legislature on or before the first Friday in July and in the possession of the governor after the first Friday in July.

Existing provisions of the Constitution prohibit the legislature from passing any bill after September 1 of an even-numbered year, except statutes calling elections, statutes providing for tax levies or appropriations for the usual current expenses of the state, urgency statutes, and bills passed after being vetoed by the governor. Until the budget bill is enacted, the legislature is prohibited, with specified exceptions, from sending the governor any bill appropriating funds for expenditure during the fiscal year of the budget bill.

AN AMENDMENT TO THE CALIFORNIA STATE
CONSTITUTION RELATING TO LEGISLATIVE
SESSIONS, SALARIES, AND EXPENSES

There is proposed to the people of the State of California that the Constitution of the State be amended as follows:

First—That Section 2 of Article IV thereof is amended to read:

SEC. 2. (a) The Senate has a membership of 40 Senators *equal to the number of members of Congress apportioned to California pursuant to federal law,* elected for 4-year terms, 20 *one-half, or as nearly as possible,* to begin every 2 years. The Assembly has a membership *equal to twice the number of Senators* ~~of 80 members~~, elected for 2-year terms. Their terms shall commence on the first Monday in December next following their election.

(b) Election of members of the Assembly shall be on the first Tuesday after the first Monday in November of even-numbered years unless otherwise prescribed by the Legislature. Senators shall be elected at the same time and places as members of the Assembly.

(c) A person is ineligible to be a member of the Legislature unless the person is an elector and has been a resident of the legislative district for one year, and a citizen of the United States and a resident of California for 3 years, immediately preceding the election.

(d) When a vacancy occurs in the Legislature the Governor immediately shall call an election to fill the vacancy.

Second—That Section 3 of Article IV thereof is amended to read:

SEC. 3. (a) The Legislature shall convene in regular session at noon on the first Monday in December of each even-numbered year and each house shall immediately organize. *The Legislature shall recess the regular session on or before the first Friday in July of each odd-numbered year, reconvene the regular session on the first Monday after the first day in January of each even-numbered year, and recess the reconvened regular session on or before the first Friday in July of the even-numbered year. The Legislature also may reconvene the regular session by a petition signed by a majority of the membership of each house that specifies the subjects to be considered, the urgency of the subjects, and the time for recess of the reconvened regular session. When the Legislature is in a regular session reconvened by petition it has power to legislate only on subjects specified in the petition.* Each session of the Legislature shall adjourn sine die by operation of the Constitution at midnight on November 30 of the following even-numbered year.

(b) On extraordinary occasions the Governor by proclamation may cause the Legislature to assemble in special session. When so assembled it has power to legislate only on subjects specified in the proclamation but may provide for expenses and other matters incidental to the session.

Third—That Section 4 of Article IV thereof is amended to read:

SEC. 4. ~~Compensation of members of the Legislature, and reimbursement for travel and living expenses in connection with their official duties, shall be prescribed by statute passed by rollcall vote entered in the journal, two-thirds of the membership of each house concurring. Commencing with 1967, in any statute enacted making an adjustment of the annual compensation of a member of the Legislature the adjustment may not exceed an amount equal to 5 percent for each calendar year following the operative date of the last adjustment, of the salary in effect when the statute is enacted. Any adjustment in the compensation may not apply until the commencement of the regular session commencing after the next general election following enactment of the statute.~~ (a) *The annual salary of a Member of the Legislature shall be the same as the annual salary of a judge of the municipal court.*

(b) *No Member of the Legislature may solicit or receive, and no person may offer or give to a Member, any honorarium, gift, or other payment that has any relationship to the Member's duties and responsibilities as a Member of the Legislature.*

(c) The Legislature may not provide retirement benefits based on any portion of a monthly salary in excess of ~~500~~ *five hundred* dollars *($500)* paid to any ~~member~~ *Member* of the Legislature unless the ~~member~~ *Member* receives the greater amount while serving as a ~~member~~ *Member* in the Legislature. The Legislature may, prior to their retirement, limit the retirement benefits payable to ~~members~~ *Members* of the Legislature who serve during or after the term commencing in 1967.

When computing the retirement allowance of the ~~member~~ *Member* who serves in the Legislature during the term commencing in 1967 or later, allowance may be made for increases in cost of living if so provided by statute, but only with respect to increases in the cost of living occurring after retirement of the ~~member~~ *Member,* except that the Legislature may provide that no ~~member~~ *Member* shall be deprived of a ~~cost of living~~ *cost-of-living* adjustment based on a monthly salary of ~~500~~ *five hundred* dollars *($500)* which has accrued prior to the commencement of the 1967 Regular Session of the Legislature.

(d) *When the Legislature is meeting in session, a Member of the Legislature may receive travel and living expenses at the same rates paid to other state officers and employees, but may receive living expenses only for days when the Member is actually in attendance at the session. During periods when the Legislature is not meeting in session, a Member may receive travel and living expenses when conducting legislative business if the Member signs a claim, under penalty of perjury, stating the reason for the expenses and that the expenses were incurred for legislative business.*

Fourth—That Section 10 of Article IV thereof is amended to read:

SEC. 10. (a) Each bill passed by the Legislature shall be presented to the Governor. It becomes a statute if it is signed by the Governor. The Governor may veto it by returning it with any objections to the house of origin, which shall enter the objections in the journal and proceed to reconsider it. If each house then passes the bill by rollcall vote entered in the journal, ~~two thirds~~ *two-thirds* of the membership concurring, it becomes a statute. A bill presented to the Governor that is not returned within 12 days becomes a statute; provided, that any bill passed by the Legislature *on or* before ~~September 1~~ *the first Friday in July* of ~~the second calendar~~ *each* year of the biennium of the legislative session and in the possession of the Governor ~~on or~~ after ~~September 1~~ *that date* that is not returned by the Governor on or before ~~September 30~~ *July 31* of that year becomes a statute. ~~The Legislature may not present to the Governor any bill after November 15 of the second calendar year of the biennium of the legislative session.~~ If the Legislature by adjournment of a special session prevents the return of a bill with the veto message, the bill becomes a statute unless the Governor vetoes the bill within 12 days by depositing it and the veto message in the office of the Secretary of State.

Any bill introduced during the first year of the biennium of the legislative session that has not been passed by the house of origin by the ~~thirtieth~~ *31st* day of January of the second calendar year of the biennium may no longer be acted on by the house. ~~No bill may be passed by either house on or after September of an even-numbered year except statutes calling elections, statutes providing for tax levies or appropriations for the usual current expenses of the State, and urgency statutes, and bills passed after being vetoed by the Governor.~~

(b) The Governor may reduce or eliminate one or more items of appropriation while approving other portions of a bill. The Governor shall amend to the bill a statement of the items reduced or eliminated with the reasons for the action. The Governor shall transmit to the house originating the bill a copy of the statement and reasons. Items reduced or eliminated shall be separately reconsidered and may be passed

Amendment B

over the Governor's veto in the same manner as bills.

Fifth—That Section 12 of Article IV thereof is amended to read:

SEC. 12. (a) Within the first 10 days of each calendar year, the Governor shall submit to the Legislature, with an explanatory message, a budget for the ensuing fiscal year containing itemized statements for recommended state expenditures and estimated state revenues. If recommended expenditures exceed estimated revenues, the Governor shall recommend the sources from which the additional revenue shall be provided.

(b) The Governor and the Governor-elect may require a state agency, officer or employee to furnish whatever information is deemed necessary to prepare the budget.

(c) The budget shall be accompanied by a budget bill itemizing recommended expenditures. The bill shall be introduced immediately in each house by the persons chairing the committees that consider appropriations. The Legislature shall pass the budget bill by midnight on June 15 of each year. Until the budget bill has been enacted, the Legislature shall not send to the Governor for consideration any bill appropriating funds for expenditure during the fiscal year for which the budget bill is to be enacted, except emergency bills recommended by the Governor or appropriations for the salaries and expenses of the Legislature.

(d) No bill except the budget bill may contain more than one item of appropriation, and that for one certain, expressed purpose. Appropriations from the General Fund of the State, except appropriations for the public schools, are void unless passed in each house by rollcall vote entered in the journal, two-thirds of the membership concurring.

(e) The Legislature may control the submission, approval, and enforcement of budgets and the filing of claims for all State agencies.

C. Proposed Constitutional Amendment Relating to Campaign Contributions

Existing provisions of the California Constitution do not provide for the regulation of the solicitation, receipt, or expenditure of campaign contributions to support or oppose candidates for state legislative office.

However, existing provisions of statutory law impose various limitations on the solicitation or receipt of campaign contributions to support candidates for elective office generally, including a requirement that an individual file a statement of his or her intention to be a candidate for an elective office with the Fair Political Practices Commission prior to the solicitation or receipt of contributions.

This measure would prohibit persons, as defined, from receiving a campaign contribution to support or oppose any individual who intends to be a candidate for a state legislative office until the time that individual has officially become a candidate for the specific state legislative office.

Existing provisions of statutory law limit the expenditure of campaign contributions by candidates generally, and limit their controlled committees to expenses associated with the election of the candidate to the specific office for which the candidate has stated his or her intention to seek, or expenses associated with holding that office.

This measure would limit the expenditure of campaign contributions made to a candidate for a specific state legislative office, or to any committee formed to support or oppose his or her candidacy, to those expenses for the defeat or the nomination or election of the candidate to the specific state legislative office for which he or she has officially become a candidate.

Existing provisions of statutory law provide for the disposition of surplus campaign funds following a post-election reporting period or the leaving of an elective office, and permit the use of those funds to make specified payments, political contributions, or donations.

This measure would require that surplus campaign funds of a candidate for a specific state legislative office or of any committee formed to support or oppose his or her candidacy which remain after the election or defeat of the candidate to be transferred to the Controller for deposit in the state's General Fund.

This measure would make a willful violation of its provisions by any person a crime punishable as a felony and would provide that a conviction of a willful violation of its provisions by an incumbent state legislative officeholder or a successful candidate for state legislative office results in a forfeiture of that office for the item to which he or she was elected. This measure would require the Attorney General to institute an action, as specified, for the forfeiture of the office.

AN AMENDMENT TO THE CALIFORNIA STATE
CONSTITUTION RELATING TO
CAMPAIGN CONTRIBUTIONS

There is proposed to the people of the State of California that the Constitution of the State be amended by adding Section 7 to Article XX, to read:

SEC. 7. (a) No person may receive a campaign contribution to support or oppose any individual who intends to be a candidate for a state legislative office until the time that individual has officially become a candidate for the specific state legislative office as provided by law.

(b) Campaign contributions made to a candidate for a specific state legislative office or to any committee formed, in whole or in part, to support or oppose his or her candidacy, whether or not the committee is controlled by the candidate, may be expended only for the nomination, election, or defeat of the candidate to that office. For purposes of this subdivision, campaign contributions made to a candidate for a specific state legislative office or to any committee formed, in whole or in part, to support or oppose his or her candidacy may not be transferred to any other candidate or to any other committee formed to support or oppose the candidacy of any other candidate for the same office or any other elective office.

(c) Any surplus campaign funds of a candidate for a

specific state legislative office or of any committee formed to support or oppose his or her candidacy which remain after the election or defeat of the candidate shall, after the payment of outstanding campaign debts, be transferred to the Controller for deposit in the State Treasury to the credit of the General Fund.

(d) Any person who willfully violates this section is guilty of a felony. Upon a conviction of a willful violation of this section by an incumbent state legislative officeholder or a successful candidate for state legislative office, he or she shall forfeit that office for the term to which he or she was elected. Notwithstanding Section 5 of Article IV, the Attorney General shall institute an action for the forfeiture of that office as provided by law for the removal from office of persons who unlawfully hold or exercise any public office.

(e) For purposes of this section:

(1) "Person" means an individual, proprietorship, firm, partnership, joint venture, syndicate, business trust, company, corporation, association, political party, committee, or labor organization.

(2) "Committee" means a combination of two or more persons acting in concert for the purpose of supporting or opposing one or more candidates for state legislative office or other elective office through the receipt of campaign contributions from two or more persons, and the expenditure of those contributions in furtherance of that purpose.

D. Proposed Constitutional Amendment Relating to the Initiative Process

Existing provisions of the California Constitution provide that an initiative measure may be proposed by presenting to the Secretary of State a petition which sets forth the proposed statute or constitutional amendment and is certified to have been signed by the requisite number of voters. It requires the Secretary of State to submit the measure at the next general or special election, as specified.

This measure would require the Secretary of State to transmit a copy of an initiative measure to the legislature, upon qualification of an initiative measure for the statewide ballot. It would require the legislature to hold and complete informational public hearings on the measure within a specified number of days of its receipt. It would require the Attorney General, the Legislative Counsel, and the Legislative Analyst to testify at the hearings, as specified.

This measure would provide that the legislature may not alter the measure or prevent it from being submitted to the voters. It would permit the legislature to make recommendations and disseminate relevant information concerning the measure. It would also provide that the requirements of this measure do not apply if an initiative petition has been signed by electors equal to twice the number otherwise required.

AN AMENDMENT TO THE CALIFORNIA STATE CONSTITUTION RELATING TO INITIATIVES

There is proposed to the people of the State of California that the Constitution of the State be amended by amending Section 8 of Article II to read:

SEC. 8. (a) The initiative is the power of the electors to propose

statutes and amendments to the Constitution and to adopt or reject them.

(b) An initiative measure may be proposed by presenting to the Secretary of State a petition that sets forth the text of the proposed statute or amendment to the Constitution and is certified to have been signed by electors equal in number to 5 percent in the case of a statute, and 8 percent in the case of an amendment to the Constitution, of the votes for all candidates for Governor at the last gubernatorial election.

(c) The Secretary of State shall then submit the measure at the next general election held at least 131 days after it qualifies or at any special statewide election held prior to that general election. The Governor may call a special statewide election for the measure.

(d) An initiative measure embracing more than one subject may not be submitted to the electors or have any effect.

(e) (1) Upon qualification of an initiative measure, the Secretary of State shall transmit a copy of the meas-

ure to the Legislature. The Legislature shall hold and complete informational public hearings concerning the measure within 30 days of November 30 of any even-numbered year, the hearings may be held after the commencement of the next regular session of the Legislature, and shall be completed within 30 days thereof.

(2) The Attorney General and the Legislative Counsel shall testify at the hearings as to any legal matters relating to the measure, including its constitutionality. Other legal experts also shall be given the opportunity to so testify. The Legislative Analyst shall prepare a fiscal analysis of the measure and shall testify at the hearings as to the fiscal implications of the measure.

(3) This subdivision does not grant the Legislature the authority to alter the measure or prevent it from being submitted to the voters. The Legislature may make recommendations and disseminate relevant information concerning the measure.

(4) The requirements of this subdivision do not apply if an initiative petition has been signed by electors equal to twice the number specified in subdivision (b).

Index

Acton, Lord, 25
Adams, John, 55
Agnos, Art, 69
Allen, Don A., 125
Aristotle, 157
Bagley, William, 17, 20–22, 55
Barkle, Dick, 145
Bell, Charles, 37
Beverly, Robert, 145
Benchley, Robert, 16
Biddick, William, 12–15
Bonaparte, Napoleon, 63, 70
Bowen, Catherine Drinker, 53, 93–94
Brandeis, Louis, 151
Broder, David A., 117–118
Brown, Edmund G., 13, 135
Brown, Jerry, 21, 110
Brown, Willie, 59–60, 121
Burton, Phil, 55–56
Bush, George, 45, 158
Calhoun, John C., 27
Carlyle, Thomas, 29
Casey, Jack, 16, 19
Cole, Clifford, 9
Collins, Larry, 107–108
Cologne, Gordon, 17, 21
Cory, Kenneth, 46
Cranston, Alan, 97
Dangerfield, Rodney, 70
Deukmejian, George, 22
Dickinson, John, 53
Douglas, Paul Howard, 95
Duffy, Gordon, 104

Eisenhower, Dwight D., 7, 8
Feldstein, Dr. Paul J., 98
Field, Mervin, 154
Finch, Robert, 100
Fitzgerald, Ernest A., 106
Flournoy, Hugh, 17, 19–21, 55
Ford, Gerald, 23
Forrest, Edward, 57
Franklin, Benjamin, 24, 55
Fuller, Thomas, 146
Garibaldi, James D., 41
Gerry, Eldridge, 46
Goldwyn, Samuel, 32
Greeley, Horace, 32
Hardy, Dr. Leroy, 46
Hayakawa, S. I., 152
Heslop, Dr. Alan, 57
Hicks, James, 16, 18
Holmes, Oliver Wendell, 4
Hoyt, Frank, 11
Hughes, Edward, 102
Humphrey, Hubert, 8–9
Humphrey, Muriel, 9
Jefferson, Thomas, 55, 118
Johnson, Hiram, 76, 85
Johnson, Leroy, 8, 9
Johnson, Ross, 107
Ketchum, William, 104
Knox, John, 16, 19, 103, 104
Lee, Eugene, 78, 84
Lake, James, 91
Leggett, Robert, 16, 18
Lincoln, Abraham, 3
Lowell, James Russell, 132

Index

Machiavelli, Niccolo, 119
Madison, James, 114
Mason, George, 34
McAllister, Leo, 29
Milias, George, 103
Miller, George, 40
Miller, George, Jr., 39–40
Mills, James, 16, 18–19
Mitchell, Greg, 107
Monagan, Ione, 12
Montesquieu, Baron de, 156, 158
Nixon, Richard, 22–23, 28, 29
Novak, Robert, 99–100
Ovid, 63
Parkhurst, John, 23
Poage, Robert, 9
Porter, Carley, 21, 103
Price, Charles, 37
Quinn, T. Anthony, 44–45, 50, 53
Reagan, Ronald, 1, 21, 103, 130, 155
Reed, Thomas, 120

Revere, Paul, 1, 157–158
Richardson, James, 93
Rockefeller, Nelson, 23
Roosevelt, Franklin D., 7, 26–27, 49
Schmitz, John, 29
Shortell, Steve, 102
Simpson, Jerry, 45
Simpson, Richard P., 78
Smirnoff, Yakov, 60
Smith, Hedrick, 91
Smith, Martin, 87–89
Torres, Arthur, 86, 93
Unruh, Jesse Marvin, 63, 88–89, 140
Veneman, Jack, 22–23, 55, 99–100
Walters, Dan, 38–39, 84
Warren, Earl, 27, 54, 140
Washington, George, 55, 105–106, 111, 116, 118, 141
Wilson, Pete, 103
Zelman, Walter, 67
Zisk, Betty, 76–77

DESIGNED BY DAVE COMSTOCK,
THIS BOOK WAS SET IN 12 POINT SABON
BY COMSTOCK BONANZA PRESS AND
DWAN TYPOGRAPHY, AND WAS
PRINTED ON GLATFELTER B-16 ACID-FREE
NATURAL PAPER BY THOMSON-SHORE, INC.